RELIGIONS TO inSPiRE

for KS3
Islam

Steve Clarke

Series editor: Steve Clarke

DYNAMIC
LEARNING

HODDER
EDUCATION
AN HACHETTE UK COMPANY

The Author and Publishers would like to thank the Chair of the Education Committee of the Muslim Council of Britain, Sheikh Dr Hojjat Ramzy for advising them on the content of this book.

It is a mark of respect in Islam to follow the name of Muhammad with (pbuh), meaning *peace be upon him*. Although this book is a secular text, it follows this convention – (pbuh) is placed after the first instance of Muhammad in each chapter – out of respect for its Muslim readers.

Although every effort has been made to ensure that website addresses are correct at time of going to press, Hodder Education cannot be held responsible for the content of any website mentioned in this book. It is sometimes possible to find a relocated web page by typing in the address of the home page for a website in the URL window of your browser.

Hachette UK's policy is to use papers that are natural, renewable and recyclable products and made from wood grown in well-managed forests and other controlled sources. The logging and manufacturing processes are expected to conform to the environmental regulations of the country of origin.

Orders: please contact Hachette UK Distribution, Hely Hutchinson Centre, Milton Road, Didcot, Oxfordshire, OX11 7HH. Telephone: +44 (0)1235 827827. Email education@hachette.co.uk Lines are open from 9 a.m. to 5 p.m., Monday to Friday. You can also order through our website: www.hoddereducation.com

© Steve Clarke 2011
First published in 2011 by
Hodder Education,
An Hachette UK Company
Carmelite House, 50 Victoria Embankment,
London EC4Y 0DZ

Impression number 11
Year 2021

Cover photo © iStockphoto/Flemming Hansen
Illustrations by Barking Dog Art, Peter Lubach, Oxford designers & Illustrators, Tony Randell
Typeset in Minion regular 12.5pt/15pt by Wooden Ark
Printed and bound by CPI Group (UK) Ltd, Croydon CR0 4YY

A catalogue record for this title is available from the British Library

ISBN: 978 1444 12216 9

Contents

1.1 Who are Muslims?

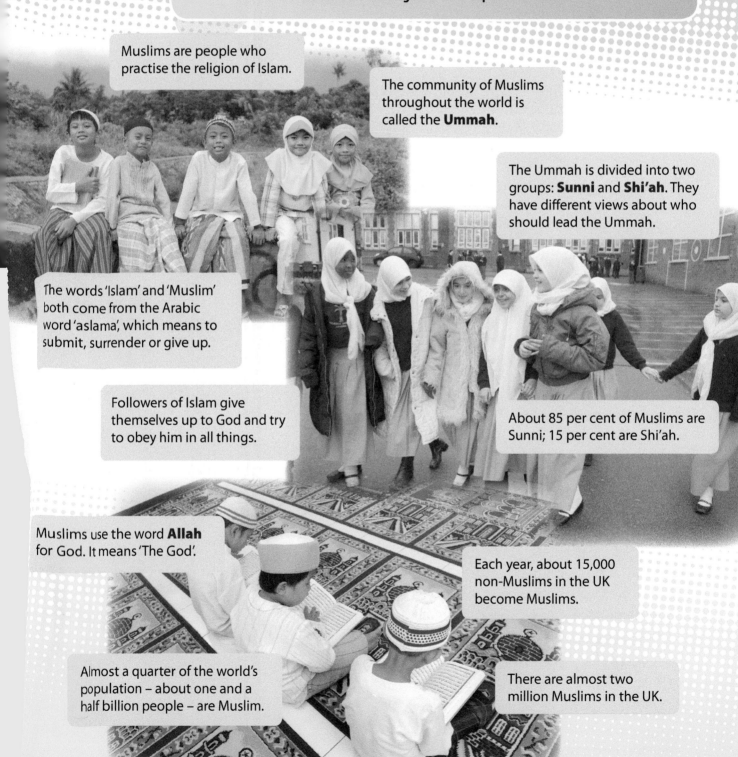

Muslims are people who practise the religion of Islam.

The community of Muslims throughout the world is called the **Ummah**.

The Ummah is divided into two groups: **Sunni** and **Shi'ah**. They have different views about who should lead the Ummah.

The words 'Islam' and 'Muslim' both come from the Arabic word 'aslama', which means to submit, surrender or give up.

Followers of Islam give themselves up to God and try to obey him in all things.

About 85 per cent of Muslims are Sunni; 15 per cent are Shi'ah.

Muslims use the word **Allah** for God. It means 'The God'.

Each year, about 15,000 non-Muslims in the UK become Muslims.

Almost a quarter of the world's population – about one and a half billion people – are Muslim.

There are almost two million Muslims in the UK.

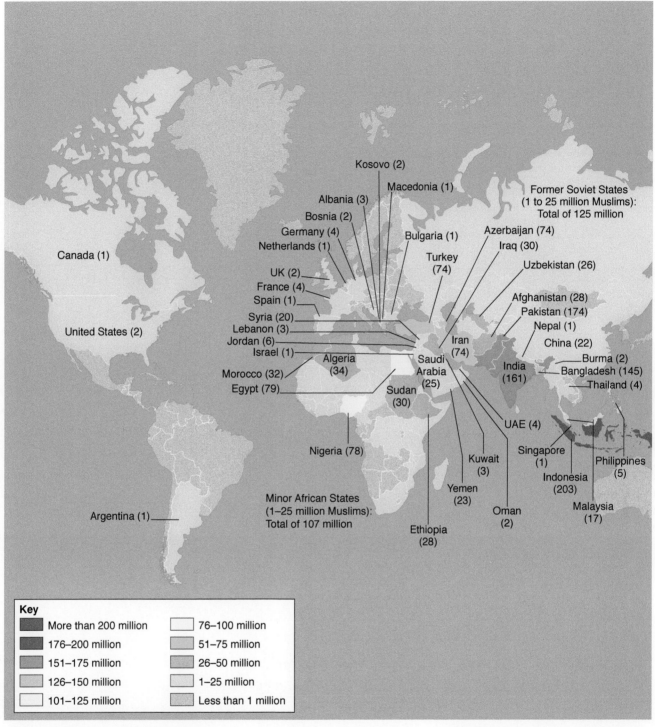

Canada (1)

United States (2)

Argentina (1)

Kosovo (2)

Macedonia (1)

Albania (3)

Bosnia (2)

Germany (4)

Netherlands (1)

Bulgaria (1)

UK (2)

France (4)

Spain (1)

Syria (20)

Lebanon (3)

Jordan (6)

Israel (1)

Algeria (34)

Morocco (32)

Egypt (79)

Turkey (74)

Azerbaijan (74)

Iraq (30)

Uzbekistan (26)

Afghanistan (28)

Pakistan (174)

Nepal (1)

China (22)

Iran (74)

India (161)

Burma (2)

Bangladesh (145)

Thailand (4)

Saudi Arabia (25)

Sudan (30)

UAE (4)

Nigeria (78)

Kuwait (3)

Yemen (23)

Oman (2)

Singapore (1)

Indonesia (203)

Malaysia (17)

Philippines (5)

Former Soviet States (1 to 25 million Muslims): Total of 125 million

Minor African States (1–25 million Muslims): Total of 107 million

Ethiopia (28)

Key

■ More than 200 million	□ 76–100 million
■ 176–200 million	□ 51–75 million
■ 151–175 million	□ 26–50 million
■ 126–150 million	□ 1–25 million
□ 101–125 million	□ Less than 1 million

Knowledge check

1 What are followers of Islam called?

2 What word do Muslims use for God?

3 What does the word Islam mean?

4 How many people follow Islam in the UK?

5 Which person is connected with the beginnings of Judaism, Christianity and Islam? (See page 6.)

This map shows the global spread of Islam. It is predicted that by 2050, there will be about three billion Muslims around the world; that will be a third of the world's population. (The figures after the country names refer to the number of Muslims in millions.)

Muslims, Jews and Christians can all trace their religions back to one man. Muslims call him Ibrahim; he is known to Jews and Christians as Abraham. Muslims refer to Jews and Christians as the 'People of the Book', because God gave his teachings to them in the Bible.

This diagram shows how the People of the Book trace their origins back to Ibrahim through Is'haq. Muslims follow Muhammad's ancestry through Isma'il.

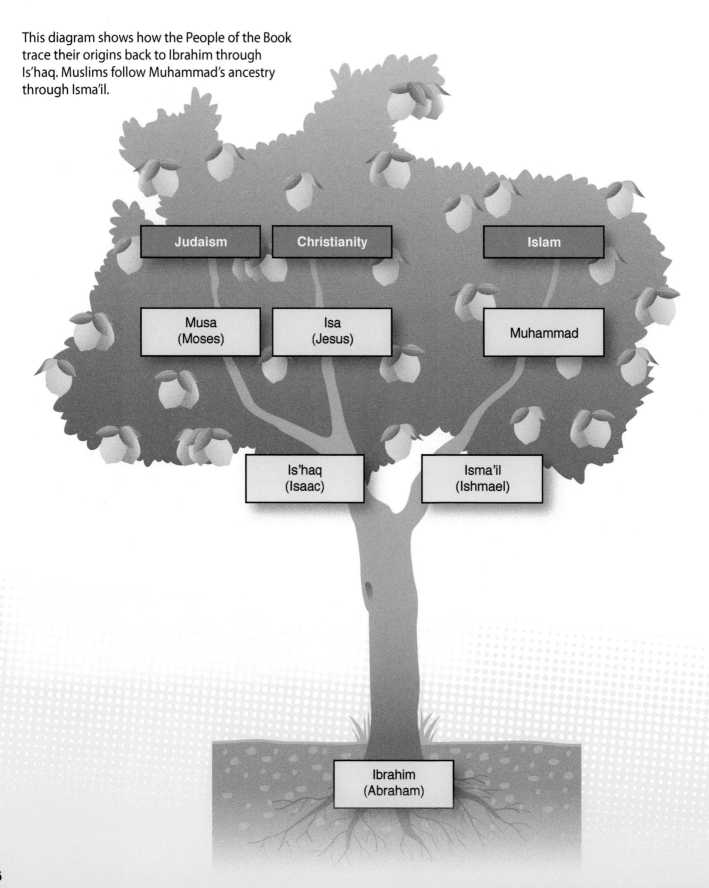

Ibrahim had two sons: Is'haq (Isaac to Jews and Christians) and Isma'il (Ishmael). Moses and Jesus were both descended from Isaac; Muhammad (pbuh) was descended from Isma'il.

Is'haq, Isa and Muhammad are all important figures in Islam. They are **prophets**. For Muslims, a prophet is someone chosen by God to teach human beings. The last and most important of the prophets was Muhammad.

The most important Muslim beliefs are that there is one God and that Muhammad is his Prophet. Stating these beliefs is called **Shahadah** (see Chapter 1.3).

1.2 What is the Qur'an?

Learning objectives

You will ...
- learn some facts about the Qur'an
- understand why the Qur'an is important to Muslims
- give advice on how to live.

The **Qur'an** is the Muslim holy book.

The Qur'an was revealed in the Arabic language.

Muslims say the words of the Qur'an have not been changed over 1400 years.

The word *Qur'an* means 'recitation'. A recitation is something read aloud or spoken from memory.

Muslims believe that the content of the Qur'an comprises the words of Allah – The God.

The Qur'an is divided into 114 chapters, called **surahs**. Each surah is divided into verses. There are 6236 verses altogether.

The words of the Qur'an were given to Muhammad (pbuh) to recite; in other words, to remember and tell others.

The first words revealed to Muhammad were: 'Read, in the name of your Lord …' (96.1)

The last words revealed to Muhammad were: 'Today I perfected your religion for you and completed My favour to you, and have chosen for you Islam as your religion.' (5.3)

The Qur'an was revealed to Muhammad over 23 years, beginning in 610CE.

Some surahs of the Qur'an are composed of beautiful Arabic poetry. They:

- stress the splendour and magnificence of Allah
- point out weaknesses in other religions that came before Islam
- describe the reward that faithful Muslims will receive
- describe the punishments that wrongdoers will receive
- tell the stories of the prophets
- confirm that Muhammad is the last and greatest of the prophets.

Other surahs are in plainer language. They:

- describe religious practices for Muslims
- establish moral rules for living
- lay down criminal laws
- give guidance about governing nations and about foreign relations
- set out rules for warfare and the treatment of captives.

Muslims say that the Qur'an is God's message to all people. It is his complete guide for living. It tells human beings what is right and what is wrong, and encourages them to do what is right and avoid what is wrong. It tells them to live together as brothers and sisters, together obeying God's will.

Muslims therefore treat the Qur'an with great respect. It is usually kept in a high place, wrapped in a cloth. When it is taken down, it is put on a wooden stand to be read from. A Muslim who reads the Qur'an will wash thoroughly first.

Muslims try to learn parts of the Qur'an by heart. Some memorise the whole of it. Such a person is called a **hafiz**, which means 'guardian': a hafiz keeps the Qur'an safe, so that it always exists, even if every copy were to be destroyed. There are about ten million hafaz (plural of hafiz) in the world.

Knowledge check

1 To whom were the words of the Qur'an first given?

2 What are its chapters called and how many are there?

3 What does the word Qur'an mean?

4 In which language was the Qur'an revealed?

5 Why are Muslims who memorise the whole of the Qur'an called guardians?

Activity A

Which facts about the Qur'an surprise you? Use them to make an illustrated guide to the Qur'an for non-Muslims, called 'Things You Didn't Know About the Qur'an'.

Activity B

1 Describe the various ways in which Muslims show their respect for the Qur'an. Why is it so important to them?

2 What is your most important possession? How do you treat it?

Activity C

Muslims believe that the Qur'an is a complete guide to life for human beings.

1 What sort of advice would you put in a guide to life?

2 If you have access to a copy of the Qur'an (there are versions in many languages on the Internet), find out some of the guidance it offers.

3 Make a 'Guide to Life' booklet containing your advice and guidance from the Qur'an that you agree with.

Activity D

1 Read the last words revealed to Muhammad. What do you think 'I perfected your religion for you' means?

2 Do you think any religion can claim to be perfect or provide a complete guide for life? Give reasons for your answer.

1.3 How and why do Muslims worship?

The Five Pillars of Islam

There are five main ways in which Muslims worship. They are called the **Five Pillars of Islam**, because they provide a framework for worship, in the same way pillars support a building.

Shahadah – A statement of belief.

Salah – Compulsory prayers, five times a day.

Zakah – Payment made annually under Islamic law to people in need.

Sawm – Fasting over a period of one month during the Islamic month of **Ramadan**.

Hajj – A pilgrimage (religious journey) to Makkah in Saudi Arabia.

Knowledge check

Match the Five Pillars of Islam with their definitions.

1 Shahadah	a	Pilgrimage to Makkah
2 Salah	b	Giving to the poor
3 Zakah	c	Statement of beliefs
4 Sawm	d	Prayer five times a day
5 Hajj	e	Fasting during Ramadan

The Shahadah

'There is no God but Allah and Muhammad is his Prophet.'

(The Shahadah)

The Shahadah must be recited with honesty and sincerity to have any meaning. If someone wants to become a Muslim, they need only repeat the Shahadah three times in front of at least two witnesses.

This is the flag of Saudi Arabia. It features the Shahadah in Arabic.

Quotations from the Qur'an

'Ramadan is the month in which the Qur'an was revealed … Whoever is not travelling must fast during that month.'

(2.185)

'You shall give to relatives, the poor, the needy, and to travellers.'

(17.26)

'Perform prayers at both ends of the day and at night-time.'

(11.114)

'There is no God but Allah.'

(3.18)

'Allah knows that you [Muhammad] are his Messenger.'

(63.1)

'And announce to the people that they will observe the pilgrimage … They will perform their duties, fulfil their promises, and visit the ancient shrine.'

(22.27, 29)

Activity A

Make a poster to illustrate the Five Pillars of Islam. Use the Arabic names, and match each of them with a quotation from the Qur'an.

Activity B

Make a PowerPoint presentation on the Shahadah. You will need to explain what it means, and go on to explain how Muslims try to act on it in their daily lives.

Activity C

The hip-hop rapper artist, Everlast, was born into a Christian family, but became a Muslim. In an interview he said, 'Islam is like gas in a car.' Explain what he meant by this, and give examples to illustrate your answer.

Activity D

'Actions are more important than beliefs.'

1 Do you think this statement is true? Give reasons for your answer.

2 What do you think a Muslim would say about this statement, and what reasons might they give?

For Muslims, worship is not separate from everyday life. They believe that everything they do should be done to please The God. The Shahadah is a statement of what Muslims believe, and the other four of the Five Pillars put those beliefs into action.

When Muslims worship, they are reminded of The God. This helps them to act in ways God wants them to act, and avoid the things that displease him.

1.4 How and why do Muslims pray?

Learning objectives

You will ...
- learn how Muslims pray
- find out what you will find in a mosque and what happens there
- understand why prayer is important to Muslims
- analyse the role of an imam.

Prayer is called salah in Arabic. Muslims pray five times a day, and each salah takes about ten minutes. They pray on a mat to ensure cleanliness.

Muslims face the **Ka'bah** when they pray. The Ka'bah is a building in Makkah, in Saudi Arabia, and is said to be the House of God on Earth.

Muslims remove their shoes and wash thoroughly before they pray in a ritual called **wudu**.

Salah consists of a sequence of actions as well as words. Each sequence is called a **rak'ah**. Muslims should perform salah regularly from the age of ten, but they are encouraged to start from the age of seven or earlier.

Before and/or after the compulsory prayers, or at any other time of the day, Muslims are encouraged to say voluntary prayers.

Knowledge check

1 Which prayer is likely to be said during a school day?
2 Between which hours should Maghrib prayers be said on 4 March 2012?
3 Which prayers might a Muslim recite at 5p.m.?
4 Which time on the prayer calendar is not the name of a prayer?

Prayer	Time	Minimum number of rak'ahs
Fajr	Between dawn (the start of daylight) and sunrise	2
Zuhr	Between midday and Asr	4
Asr	Mid-afternoon until just before sunset	4
Maghrib	Between sunset and dusk (the end of daylight)	3
Isha	Between dusk and midnight (some say before Fajr)	4

This table shows prayer times.

March	Day	Fajr (Dawn)	Shorouk (Sunrise)	Zuhr (Noon)	Asr (Afternoon)	Maghrib (Sunset)	Isha (Dusk)
1	Thu	4:57	6:54	12:19	3:06	5:44	7:42
2	Fri	4:54	6:51	12:18	3:07	5:46	7:44
3	Sat	4:52	6:49	12:18	3:08	5:48	7:46
4	Sun	4:50	6:47	12:18	3:10	5:50	7:48
5	Mon	4:47	6:44	12:18	3:11	5:52	7:50
6	Tue	4:45	6:42	12:18	3:12	5:54	7:52
7	Wed	4:42	6:40	12:17	3:14	5:56	7:54

This table shows the type of chart a Muslim would consult to get the exact times for prayer in a given week.

Praying at times throughout the day reminds Muslims that God is constantly with them and of their submission to him and duty to praise him. This means that they are encouraged to do good and avoid evil. Through prayer, they ask God for guidance, express gratitude, and ask for help in making difficult decisions.

On Fridays, instead of offering the Zuhr prayers, it is obligatory for Muslim men to attend **Jumu'ah prayers** at a place of worship – the mosque. It is optional for women to attend.

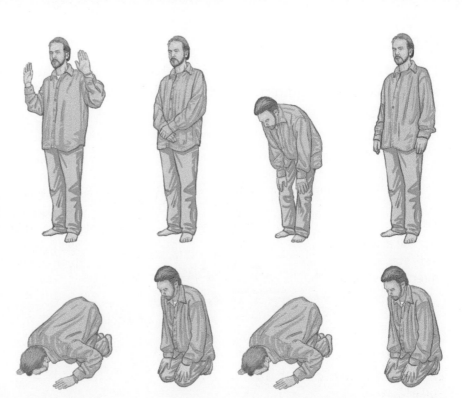

A rak'ah.

Jumu'ah prayers

1 About fifteen minutes before the salah, there is a call to prayer – the **adhan**. This is amplified to be heard by everyone in the area.

2 There is a second adhan as the leader of the congregation – the **imam** – is about to start his talk.

3 The imam delivers two sermons.

4 Jumu'ah prayers are shorter than Zuhr, consisting of only two rak'ahs.

5 Communal prayers.

Qiblah wall in the mosque

The **qiblah**, which means 'direction' in Arabic, is a mark on the wall that indicates the direction of the Ka'bah in Makkah.

Minaret
A thin tower from which the adhan is called.

Minbar
A staircase where the imam stands to address the community.

Washing area
Muslims perform wudu before praying, so mosques have a place to do this. It may be inside or outside the mosque.

Mihrab
A small alcove that indicates which direction is the qiblah.

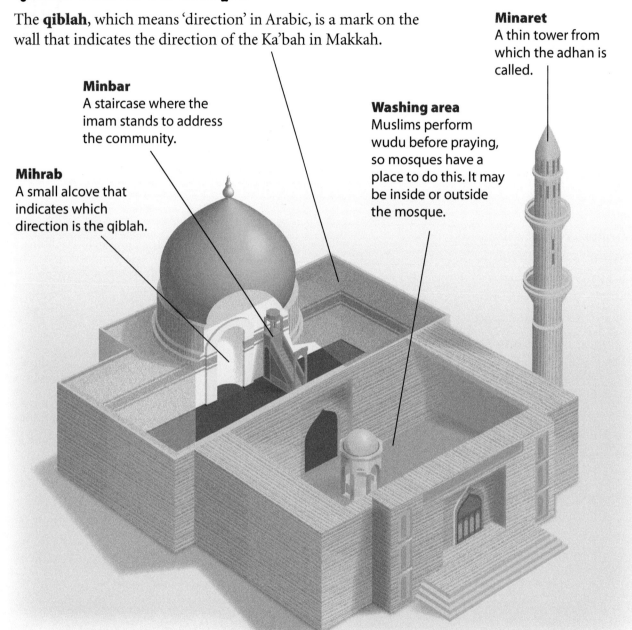

Many mosques are more than just places to pray. In this country, some are called Islamic Centres, because they may also contain:

- a sports hall
- a café
- a social centre
- a school for studying the Qur'an or Arabic
- an information centre.

Knowledge check

1 What should Muslims do before they pray?

2 Which prayers are said in the mosque around midday on Fridays?

3 Who is supposed to attend?

4 Who usually leads the salah?

5 How do Muslims know which way to face when praying in a mosque?

6 As well as prayer, what are mosques sometimes used for?

Activity A

Imagine you are an architect. You have been asked to design a mosque for your town or city.

1 Draw a plan (overhead map – see an example below) of your design, and a drawing of the outside.

2 Label each part to indicate what it is used for.

3 Remember that many mosques are not used for just praying.

Activity B

Make an information leaflet called 'A Guide to salah'. You will need to describe how a Muslim prays, with illustrations, and explain why it is important.

An overhead map of a mosque – can you name the different sections?

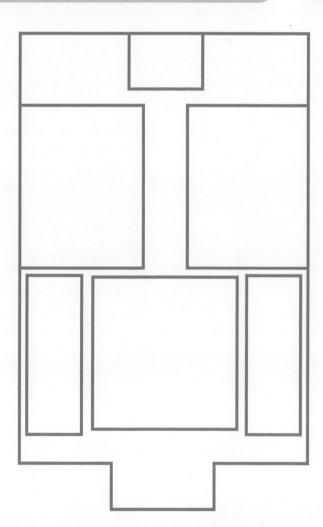

Activity C

Find out more about the role of the imam in Muslim communities.

1 Think of questions you would like to ask; then conduct some research in order to be able to answer them.

2 If there is a mosque near your school, you may be able to use your questions in an interview with the imam.

Activity D

The five set prayers are said to be **fard** (compulsory); nafil prayers are personal prayers and optional.

1 Do you think one is more important than the other? Give reasons for your answer.

2 What reasons might someone put forward for having a different opinion?

1.5 Why do Muslims go to Makkah?

Learning objectives

You will ...
- find out what happens on Hajj
- understand why Hajj is important for Muslims
- think about the benefits of going on Hajj.

Makkah is a city in Saudi Arabia, and is considered by Muslims to be the holiest place in the world. Muhammad (pbuh) was born there in 570CE, but the reason why it is so sacred is that it contains a cube-shaped structure called the **Ka'bah** (which means 'the Cube').

One of the Five Pillars is a requirement for every Muslim to undertake a pilgrimage – a religious journey – to Makkah. They should do this at least once in their lifetime, providing they are physically able and can afford to.

Pilgrims – called Hajjis – undertake a number of ritual activities over the five days, from the eighth to the twelfth of the Muslim month of Dhu al-Hijjah.

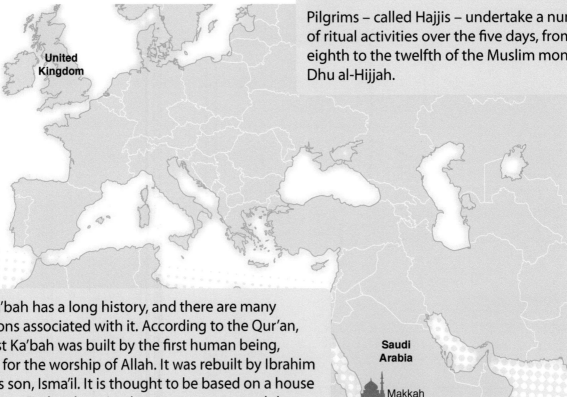

The Ka'bah has a long history, and there are many traditions associated with it. According to the Qur'an, the first Ka'bah was built by the first human being, Adam, for the worship of Allah. It was rebuilt by Ibrahim and his son, Isma'il. It is thought to be based on a house in heaven. Today there is a large mosque around the Ka'bah – Masjid al-Haram (**masjid** means mosque).

For Muslims, the Ka'bah is sacred because it is the house of The God (Allah). For this reason, Makkah is such a holy city that non-Muslims are not allowed to enter.

Preparation for the Hajj

One of the purposes of Hajj is to bring Muslims closer together, so people tend to go in groups to share the experience with each other. During the Hajj, men are required to wear **ihram**.

Ihram consists of two simple pieces of white cloth to cover the top and bottom halves of the body. Women are simply required to dress modestly. Wearing a simple uniform stresses the oneness of the Ummah, and shows that everyone – regardless of ethnic background, wealth or nationality – is equal.

While wearing ihram, Muslims must practise self-control. They should not shave, cut their nails, wear perfume, swear, quarrel, lie, have sexual relations, damage plants, cover the head (for men) or the face and hands (for women), marry, wear shoes over the ankles, or carry weapons. By dressing and living simply, without material comforts, the pilgrims feel closer to God.

Knowledge check

1 Around which city do the events of Hajj take place?

2 Why is the Ka'bah sacred to Muslims?

3 Where is the Ka'bah located?

4 What do male pilgrims wear?

5 How long does the Hajj last?

Men must change into ihram clothes before they start their Hajj.

Rituals

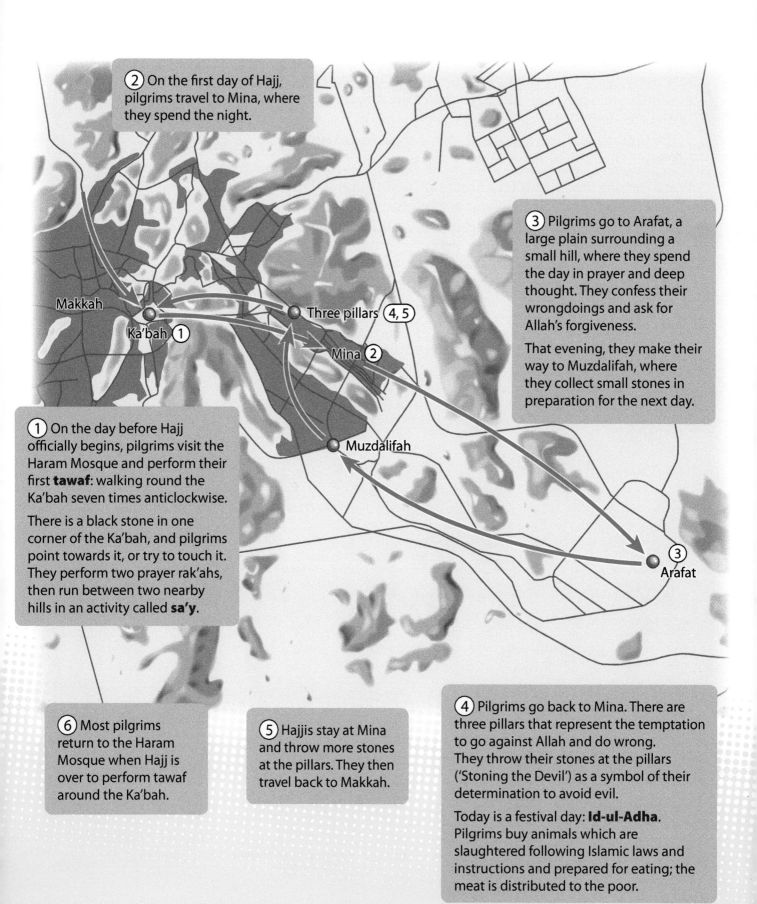

② On the first day of Hajj, pilgrims travel to Mina, where they spend the night.

③ Pilgrims go to Arafat, a large plain surrounding a small hill, where they spend the day in prayer and deep thought. They confess their wrongdoings and ask for Allah's forgiveness.

That evening, they make their way to Muzdalifah, where they collect small stones in preparation for the next day.

Makkah

Ka'bah ①

Three pillars ④, ⑤

Mina ②

Muzdalifah

Arafat ③

① On the day before Hajj officially begins, pilgrims visit the Haram Mosque and perform their first **tawaf**: walking round the Ka'bah seven times anticlockwise.

There is a black stone in one corner of the Ka'bah, and pilgrims point towards it, or try to touch it. They perform two prayer rak'ahs, then run between two nearby hills in an activity called **sa'y**.

⑥ Most pilgrims return to the Haram Mosque when Hajj is over to perform tawaf around the Ka'bah.

⑤ Hajjis stay at Mina and throw more stones at the pillars. They then travel back to Makkah.

④ Pilgrims go back to Mina. There are three pillars that represent the temptation to go against Allah and do wrong. They throw their stones at the pillars ('Stoning the Devil') as a symbol of their determination to avoid evil.

Today is a festival day: **Id-ul-Adha**. Pilgrims buy animals which are slaughtered following Islamic laws and instructions and prepared for eating; the meat is distributed to the poor.

AL-HIDAAYAH'S 2010 (1431)

HAJJ TOUR

Your journey of a lifetime begins here…

CALL **0845 456 0845**

Lines open 9.30am to 5.30pm on weekdays,
and 9.30am to 1pm on Saturday.

Al-Hidaayah Travel Ltd

436 Coventry Road   Tel: 0845 456 0845
Small Heath   Fax: 0121 753 2422
Birmingham B10 0UG   Email: hajj@al-hidaayah.co.uk

www.al-hidaayah.travel

Makkah

There are specialist travel agents who can arrange Hajj.

Knowledge check

1 What is tawaf?

2 What do pilgrims do on the Plain of Arafat?

3 On which day do Muslims sacrifice an animal?

Activity A

There are many travel companies that specialise in taking Muslims on Hajj. Design a leaflet or small brochure that a tour organisation could use to advertise their services and inform potential customers what Hajj is about.

Activity B

'*And proclaim to mankind the Hajj …
that they may witness things that are of
benefit to them.*'

(Qur'an 22.27–28)

Imagine you are on Hajj. Write a diary describing your experiences, and explaining why you perform the rituals.

Activity C

Malcolm X was an American Muslim. He went on Hajj in 1964, and wrote to his friends and colleagues: 'There were tens of thousands of pilgrims, from all over the world. They were of all colors [sic], from blue-eyed blondes to black-skinned Africans. But we were all participating in the same ritual, displaying a spirit of unity and brotherhood that my experiences in America had led me to believe never could exist.'

How do the rituals of Hajj create a 'spirit of unity and brotherhood'?

Activity D

'The Hajj is just symbolic. None of the activities can actually change a person's life.'

1 Do you agree with this statement?

2 What reasons would a Muslim have for disagreeing?

1.6 Why do Muslims fast?

Learning objectives

You will ...
- learn what it means to fast during Ramadan
- understand why fasting is important for Muslims
- analyse the benefits of fasting for Muslims.

Sawm (fasting) during the month of Ramadan is one of the Five Pillars of Islam.

During Ramadan, fasting takes place during daylight hours.

Fasting means not eating, drinking, smoking or making love.

Some Muslims try to read the whole of the Qur'an during Ramadan.

Ramadan is the ninth month of the Islamic year.

During Ramadan, people wish each other *Ramadan Mubarak* – 'Blessed Ramadan' and sometimes send greetings cards.

People who are travelling need not fast while they are travelling, but should fast later.

It is believed that the first verses of the Qur'an were revealed to Prophet Muhammad (pbuh) during the month of Ramadan.

Elderly and seriously ill people do not have to fast, but should give to the poor instead. Pregnant women need not fast if it will harm their health or that of their unborn baby.

When the fast is broken at sunset, families have a simple meal together, often starting with dates as the Prophet used to (**Iftar**).

There are other voluntary fasting days, but only in Ramadan is fasting a requirement.

Knowledge check

1 What is Ramadan?
2 What is special about Ramadan?
3 What must Muslims not do during daylight hours in Ramadan?
4 Who need not fast during Ramadan?
5 Which festival follows Ramadan?

What's the point of fasting?

'The reason Muslims fast is to discipline their body and mind. The absence of food and drink and other pleasures provides a perfect opportunity to concentrate on prayer and worship. Not having the luxuries of life to hand makes it easier to reflect on life and be grateful for what we do have. Muslims use this month to start afresh and give their life a new direction.'

Adam Yosef, a Muslim from Birmingham. (BBC website)

At the end of Ramadan

Muslims celebrate a successful fast with a festival called **Id-ul-Fitr**. Many attend a congregational Id prayer in the morning after sunrise, then they celebrate Id. It lasts for three days. It is forbidden to fast at Id; so, on the first morning after the month of Ramadan, families will have a light breakfast together. They may decorate their homes, and exchange cards and presents.

This is the biggest Iftar in the world. It takes place every evening during Ramadan at the Masjid al-Haram in Makkah.

- More than 12,000 metres of tablecloth are stretched out for the Iftar.
- It costs about 1 million Saudi riyals (£165,000) each day.
- The number of dates consumed daily by worshippers in the Holy Mosque is estimated to be more than 5 million.
- Roughly 1.2 million people attend each day.
- It takes no more than fifteen minutes from putting out the tablecloths to clearing up afterwards.

Activity A

Imagine you are a web designer, working on a website to provide information for primary school children about Islam. Write a FAQ page for the site on sawm and Ramadan.

Activity B

1 Imagine you are the parent of a child in Year 6 of a British school – Mr or Mrs Rahman. Your child (Deepak – son; Deepon – daughter) is the only Muslim in the school and is about to fast for the first time.

2 Write a letter to the school's headteacher to explain what sawm is all about.

Activity C

Abu Huraira related that Rasulullah [i.e. Muhammad] said: 'Many people who fast get nothing from their fast except hunger and thirst, and many people who pray at night get nothing from it except wakefulness.'
(Hadith – one of a collection of sayings of Muhammad)

1 What does this Hadith mean? You will need to explain what sawm means and why it is carried out during Ramadan.

2 You will need to go on to analyse how sawm may bring benefits for a Muslim.

Activity D

1 Research how Id-ul-Fitr is celebrated in different countries. Look for historical as well as cultural reasons for the differences.

2 Try to explain the feelings that Muslims may experience during the celebrations, and how they express them. You could present your findings to the rest of the class.

1.7 What happens when Muslims are born?

Learning objectives

You will …
- learn about the ceremonies that take place after a Muslim baby is born
- understand why these ceremonies are important for Muslims
- link your learning about Muslim birth ceremonies with other things you have learnt about Islam.

Here are Malik and Hanan.

Assalamu alaikum

You reply:
'Wa alaikum assalam'.

This is how Muslims greet each other. Malik and Hanan have said 'Peace be with you,' and you have replied, 'And peace be with you.'

They are thrilled: they have recently had a baby boy. They have named him Ali.

As soon as our baby was born, I whispered the adhan in his right ear.

So the first words that our baby heard were about the greatness of Allah. This is an invitation to submit to God and worship him. We believe this will protect him from evil.

THE ADHAN

Allahu Akbar
God is great (four times)
Ash-hadu al-la ilaha illallah
I bear witness that there is no God except the one God. (twice)
Ash-hadu anna Muhammadan Rasulullah
I bear witness that Muhammad is the messenger of God (twice)
Hayya 'ala-salah
Come to prayer (twice)
Hayya 'ala-l-falah
Come to worship (twice)
Allahu Akbar
God is Great (twice)
La ilaha illallah
There is no God except the One God (once)

I softened a small piece of date in my mouth and rubbed it onto the baby's lips and gums. This is a sunnah, a tradition given to us by the Holy Messenger (pbuh). It is called tahnik.

The Prophet (pbuh) used to do tahnik when newborn babies were presented to him. It gives the baby sugar, for energy. As he swallows, it strengthens his jaws and gets him ready for breastfeeding. It is also a symbol of our wish for him to have a sweet and pleasant life.

On the seventh day after the birth, we held an aqiqah ceremony. In the first part of the ceremony, little Ali's hair was shaved from his head. It is sunnah to weigh the hair and give the same weight in silver to the poor. Actually, we gave money.

After that we officially gave Ali his name. We chose it carefully; it means 'noble'. That's what we hope he will grow up to be.

It is also sunnah to sacrifice two lambs and distribute the meat, giving some to the poor and some to share with our family and friends. A Muslim butcher arranged this for us, and gave us the fleeces to remember the occasion.

Another sunnah is to circumcise a boy before he is twelve years old. Circumcision involves removing the foreskin of his penis. We chose to circumcise Ali shortly after his aqiqah. We thought that, being so young, he would heal more quickly. It is a sign that he is a Muslim, he is part of the Ummah.

Knowledge check

1 What are the first words a Muslim baby hears?

2 What is sunnah?

3 What is tahnik?

4 Why is a baby's cut hair weighed?

5 Apart from tahnik, what other two sunnahs take place after the birth of a baby boy?

Activity A

Design an aqiqah invitation card. Provide information inside so that your guests will know what will happen, and why. Don't forget to invite them to the aqiqah meal. Try to find some Hadith that explain the different parts of the ceremony.

Activity C

'The ceremonies that take place after the birth of a baby are more for the parents' benefit than the child's.'

1 Explain what reasons a person may have for agreeing with this statement, and why someone may disagree.

2 Use the information from this chapter and your own research to describe the benefits of the birth ceremonies from a Muslim point of view. Which of these benefits are for the parents, and which for the baby?

Activity B

Make a PowerPoint presentation to explain how Muslim children are brought up in submission to God. You could include the following sections:

- The birth of a baby.
- Learning the beliefs of Islam.
- Learning from the Qur'an.
- Learning to worship.

Activity D

When a baby is born to Muslim parents, it is said to be a Muslim. Do you agree that parents should decide the faith in which to bring up their child, or should the child be free to make up its own mind? Try to present both sides of the argument.

The big assignment

Task

To produce an information and guidance pack that identifies some of the difficulties Muslim pupils may have practising their faith in Britain, and suggests some solutions or ways that the difficulties could be lessened.

Objectives

- To research the religious practices that young Muslims are required to perform.
- To consider the challenges young Muslims may face in trying to follow their faith in a non-Muslim culture.
- To suggest ways that changes could be made to make religious practice easier.

Outcome

To produce an information and guidance pack of leaflets that could be used in the local community to help young Muslims to practise their faith.

You should include information about:

- the Ummah and Muslim values
- learning in a Madrasah (an Islamic school where Muslims study the Qur'an)
- the Five Pillars
- salah
- sawm and Ramadan
- Hajj.

You could also include information about the values that non-Muslim children are brought up to hold.

Guidance

1   Work in groups of six or seven people. Each person should be given a specific job to do, and the rest of the group should support them in doing it.

2   Pupils who are Muslims could act as advisers to the groups.

3   Take one topic each, and conduct some thorough factual research.

4   Think about possible problems a Muslim may face in relation to your topic in Britain today.

5   Think of ways these problems could be resolved. For example, for salah:
   • Describe how and why Muslims perform salah.
   • Outline some of the difficulties a young Muslim may have practising salah (for example, Zuhr prayers, possible racial bullying, interrupted sleep).
   • Suggest possible solutions, such as access to a room in school for prayer.

6   Each member of the group should write up their topic in the form of an information and guidance leaflet.

7   The leaflets should be agreed by the other members of the group.

8   As a group, compile a short questionnaire to ask your parent(s) or guardian(s) about the values that you are brought up to respect.

   Include questions about how you were taught about table manners, politeness, right and wrong, making friends, talking to adults and things that your parent(s) or guardian(s) think are important for you to know.

9   Each person in the group should conduct the survey at home.

10 The group together should analyse the answers to the questionnaire and compile a summary sheet. Try to come up with a 'top ten' list of values that you can compare with the values of the Ummah.

11 If you have an inclusion officer in your school, present your completed pack to them and ask their opinion on it.

Assessment

You will be assessed on:

✓ how well you use specialist vocabulary

✓ the accuracy of your accounts of Muslim practices

✓ your ability to explain the importance of them

✓ your ability to show empathy with young Muslims in Britain.

2.1 What do Muslims believe?

Learning objectives

You will ...
- learn the seven main beliefs of Islam
- understand how they may affect the life of a Muslim
- consider your beliefs along with Muslim beliefs.

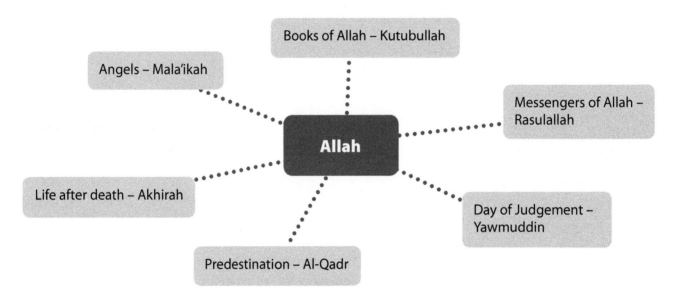

The seven main beliefs of Islam.

Muslims believe in ...

1 ... the God – *Allah*

'He is Allah, the One. Allah is eternal and absolute. None is born of him, nor is he born. And there is none like him.'

(Surah 112.1–4)

Tawhid means the oneness of Allah. Muslims believe that he is **omniscient** (all-knowing), **omnibenevolent** (completely good), **omnipotent** (all-powerful). He is **omnipresent** (with us all the time). He provides for people and takes care of their needs. He gives life and he takes it away. We return to him after death.

2 ... Angels – *Mala'ikah*

'Angels are appointed over you to protect you; they are kind and honourable, and write down your deeds. They know and understand all that you do.'

(Surah 82.10–12)

Angels are not physical beings, but have been created by Allah out of light and cannot be seen. Unlike humans, they do not have free will: they can never disobey Allah.

Muslims believe that angels are in constant contact with humans, watching over them, especially when they pray. The angels record everything a person does.

3 ... the books of Allah – *Kutubullah*

Allah's guidance is contained in his holy books.

- *Tawrah of Musa* (the Torah of Moses)
- *Zabur of Dawud* (the Psalms of David)
- *Injil of Isa* (the Gospel of Jesus)
- The *Qur'an* as revealed to Muhammad (pbuh).

Only the Qur'an contains Allah's guidance in its original form.

4 ... the messengers of Allah – *Rusulullah*

'This Muhammad is a messenger of the series of messengers of old.'

(Surah 53.56)

Through his messengers and prophets, Allah provides people with guidance so that they can lead good lives. There are said to have been 124,000 messengers and prophets in history, and the Qur'an mentions 25 by name.

Muslims believe that Muhammad was the last of the prophets: there will be no more after him. He is thought to be the greatest of the prophets because the message given through him contains all the messages of the previous prophets.

Muslims believe that the first five books of the Jewish Bible and the Gospel of the Christian Bible are based on the message of God. Only the Qur'an has the true message.

5 ... the Day of Judgement – *Yawmuddin*

'If Allah punished people according to what they deserved, he would not leave on earth a single living thing.'

(Surah 16.61)

Muslims believe that Allah created the universe, and on the Day of Judgement will destroy it.

The end of the world will be marked by a blinding light cutting through the sky. The moon and stars will disappear, mountains will crumble to dust and the seas will boil. The dead will rise, and everyone will be asked to explain everything they have done in life.

6 ... Predestination – *Al-Qadr*

'Nobody knows what they will earn tomorrow, nor does anyone know in what land they are to die. Only Allah has full knowledge and is acquainted with all things.'

(Surah 31.34)

Muslims believe that Allah is the absolute controller of the universe. Everything happens because Allah wants it to happen, and nothing happens that he does not want to happen. So everything is **predestined**.

However, humans do not know what their destinies are. So they can choose the course of their lives, even though Allah knows what choices they will make in advance.

Muhammad was once asked why people should bother doing good deeds, if everything is predestined. The Prophet replied: 'Do you know what has been decided for you?'

7 ... Life after death – *Akhirah*

'Everyone shall taste death. And only on the Day of Resurrection shall you receive what you are due … The life of this world is only the enjoyment of deception.'

(Surah 3.185)

Muslims believe that life on earth is not an end in itself: it is the cause of reward or punishment in the afterlife.

People will be rewarded for their good actions by living in paradise. This is a place of peace, purity and love. Wrongdoers will be sent to hell. Allah only sends people there as a last resort.

Knowledge check

1 What does Tawhid mean?
2 What do angels do?
3 Which book contains God's full message?
4 What do God's messengers do?
5 What is predestination?
6 What is paradise like?

These Muslims on Hajj are asking Allah's forgiveness. They believe the Day of Judgement will be like this.

Activity A

Make a wallchart that could be displayed in a primary school classroom to show six and seven year olds what Muslims believe.

Activity B

Write an account of what Muslims believe. How and why might their beliefs affect the way they live their lives?

Activity C

1 What do Muslims believe about life after death?

2 Do you believe that there is life after death? Give reasons for your answers.

3 Do you have to be religious to believe in life after death? Give reasons for your answers.

Activity D

1 Do you believe that the course of your life has been set in advance, or do you think that you have control over it?

2 If human beings were not in control of their lives, would a criminal be responsible for his or her actions?

3 If there is a God who knows and controls everything, how could he allow suffering?

4 Give reasons for your answers, and suggest what answers a Muslim might give.

2.2 Who was Muhammad (pbuh)?

Learning objectives

You will ...
- learn about the life of Muhammad
- understand why Muhammad is important to Muslims
- analyse the impact Muhammad has on the lives on Muslims.

Muslims believe that Islam started when God gave his final message for human beings to Muhammad. The message became the Qur'an. Muslims consider Muhammad to be the last and the greatest messenger of God.

As he grew up, he became known for his honesty, generosity and wisdom.

His father died just before he was born and his mother died six years later; he was brought up first by his grandfather and then by his uncle, Abu Talib.

Muhammad was born in Makkah in the year 570CE in what is today Saudi Arabia.

Makkah was a city of rogues and cheats, and Muhammad hated the dishonesty and criminality he saw.

After Muhammad's death, the revelations were collected together to form the Qur'an.

محمد

Muhammad took to meditating in the Cave of Hira, near the top of Jabal al-Nur, the 'Mountain of Light' near Makkah.

Muhammad received further messages over a period of 23 years.

When Muhammad was about 40, the Angel Jibril gave him his first message from God.

The calligraphy in the centre of this page is the name of the Prophet written in Arabic.

Knowledge check

1 When was Muhammad born?

2 In which country is Makkah today?

3 Who brought Muhammad up?

4 What upset Muhammad about Makkah?

5 How long did it take for the Qur'an to be revealed to Muhammad?

6 For which city did Muhammad leave Makkah? (See page 32.)

Calligraphy of the word 'Allah' in En-Nasir mosque in Egypt.

Muhammad's family and friends became his first disciples – the first Muslims. He preached the messages he received to the people of Makkah, but they rejected and ridiculed him. When Muhammad criticised the people for their dishonesty and injustice, they turned against him.

However, the people of Yathrib, a city some 350 kilometres away, were impressed by Muhammad's claims to be the Messenger of God, and invited him to live with them. Muhammad accepted, and renamed it Madinatu'n Nabi – the City of the Prophet. Today it is known as al-Madinah.

The Hijrah

Muhammad's departure from Makkah to Yathrib took place in 622CE, and is called the **Hijrah**. Muslims see it as the key moment in the development of Islam. In fact, the Muslim dating system starts at that point. So the year 622CE is the year 1AH (after Hijrah) in the Muslim calendar.

Although Muhammad conquered Makkah in 630CE, he continued to live in al-Madinah. He died there in 632CE.

Many Muslims say or write the words 'Peace be upon him' after the name of a prophet as a mark of respect. It is usually shortened to pbuh. In Arabic, this is called salawat, and can be shortened to SAW.

Activity A

Read the account of Muhammad's life. At which points in his life would he have felt the following emotions?

- humiliated
- excited
- happy
- angry
- lonely
- peaceful
- scared
- wanted

Pilgrims go to Jabal al-Nur, the Mountain of Light, at the top of which is the sacred Hira cave, where Muhammad received his first message from God.

What does Muhammad mean to Muslims today?

He was the last prophet of God.

He received the Qur'an, God's greatest gift to the world.

He taught us the Qur'an without changing one word of it. Not only did he teach the Qur'an: he lived it.

Although we do not worship him, he was an exemplary human being – one we should try to be like.

'Muhammad is no more than a messenger, and indeed (many) messengers have passed away before him.'

(Surah 3.144)

'We have sent you, Muhammad, as a witness, as a bearer of glad tidings, and as a warner, in order that you, mankind, may believe in Allah and his Messenger, and that you assist and honour him, and that you glorify Allah's praises morning and afternoon.'

(Surah 48.8–9)

Activity B

Read a detailed account of Muhammad receiving the Qur'an in the Cave of Hira. After this revelation, Muhammad hurried home and told his wife, Khadijah, what had happened.

1 With a partner, role play the scene between Muhammad and Khadijah. Think about his emotional state, and what Khadijah would think about what had happened.

2 Now write a script based on your role play.

Activity C

1 Write a set of questions that you would ask Muhammad about his experiences, if you had the chance. Divide them into these categories:

- Questions about his childhood in Makkah and how it prepared him for adulthood.
- Questions about the revelation of the Qur'an.
- Questions about being a prophet of God.

2 Conduct some research to try to answer your questions.

Activity D

Look at the quotes from the Surah, and the speech bubbles. In what ways is Muhammad more than a role model for Muslims?

2.3 What are the Abrahamic faiths?

Learning objectives

You will ...
- find out which religions are the Abrahamic faiths
- understand why they are called the Abrahamic faiths
- learn why Jerusalem is special to all three faiths
- understand what the faiths have in common
- analyse some stories associated with Jerusalem.

Jerusalem

The city of Jerusalem is the capital city of Israel. The name Jerusalem comes from Hebrew, the language of Judaism. It means the 'Home of Peace'. It is unique as a city, because it is special to three religions: Judaism, Christianity and Islam. In Arabic, it is called Al-Quds, which means the 'Holy Sanctuary'.

It is special to Jews because it contains the site of the Jewish Temple, destroyed in 70CE by the Romans. The Temple was never rebuilt, and all that remains of it is its Western Wall. This is a holy place for Jews, a site of pilgrimage and prayer.

Jesus spent the last week of his life in Jerusalem, and it was there that, according to Christians, he was killed and later rose from death back to life. The Church of the Holy Sepulchre covers the place where tradition has it Jesus was crucified and buried.

This photo was taken at around 3a.m. and shows the thousands of Jews who come to pray at the Western Wall in the days running up to the Day of Atonement – the holiest day in the Jewish calendar.

Knowledge check

1 What does the word Jerusalem mean?

2 What is Jerusalem known as in Arabic?

3 What do Jews do at the Western Wall?

4 What does the Church of the Holy Sepulchre commemorate?

According to Islamic tradition, around the year 621CE, Muhammad (pbuh) was transported by God from the Masjid al-Haram in Makkah to the Masjid-ul-Aqsa (the Farthest Mosque) in Jerusalem. He was carried on a mythological horse called Buraq.

At the Masjid-ul-Aqsa, Muhammad led the other prophets in prayer before being taken by Buraq to heaven, where he received instructions from Allah about the number of salah. He was returned to Makkah the same night.

A mosque called the Masjid-ul-Aqsa was built on the site of the Jewish Temple to commemorate the Night Journey. The rock on which Muhammad is said to have led prayers was covered in 689CE by the Dome of the Rock.

The Noble Sanctuary

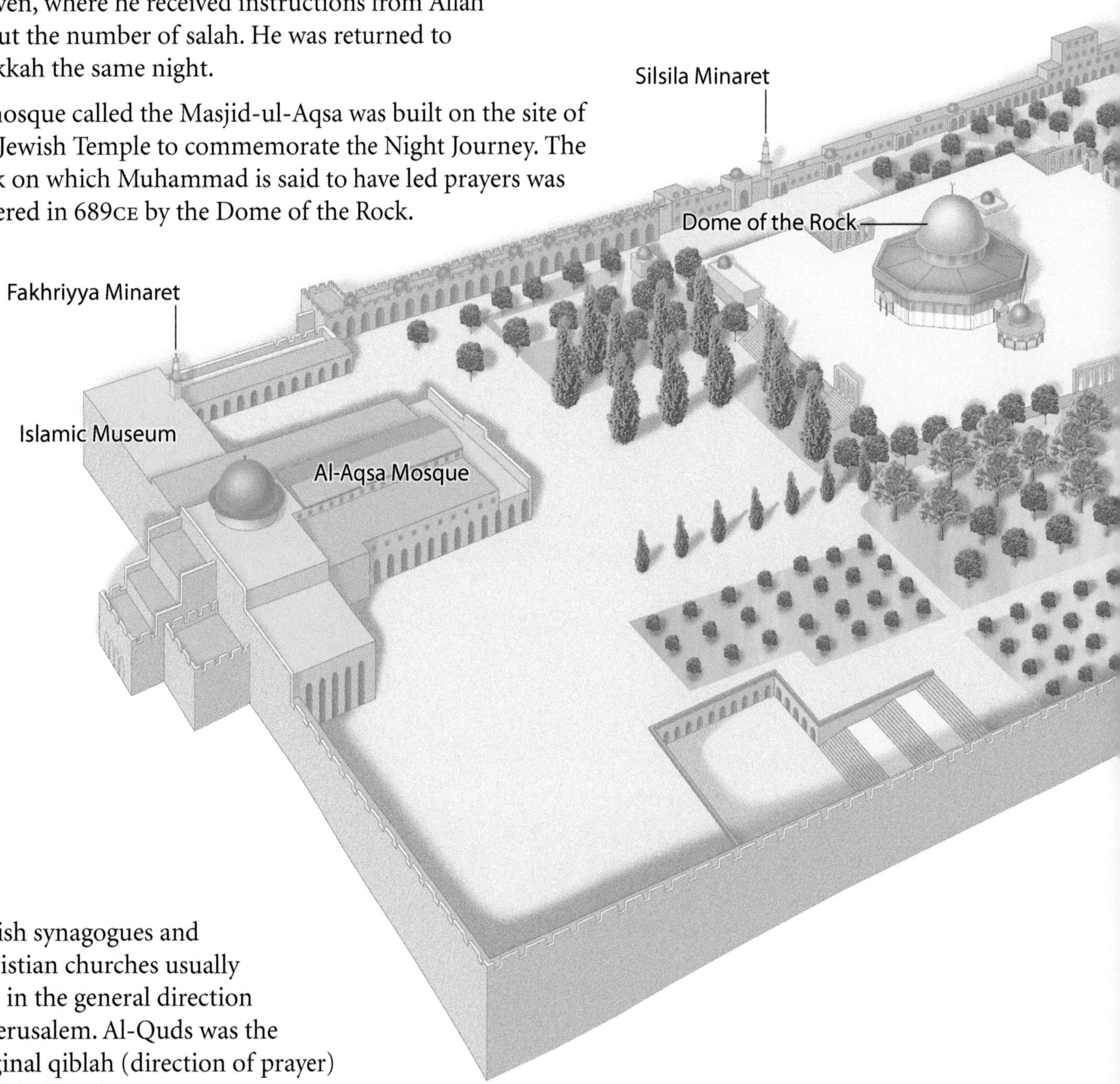

Silsila Minaret

Dome of the Rock

Fakhriyya Minaret

Islamic Museum

Al-Aqsa Mosque

Jewish synagogues and Christian churches usually face in the general direction of Jerusalem. Al-Quds was the original qiblah (direction of prayer) for Muslims from 610 to 623CE, when Prophet Muhammad received an instruction from God to face the Ka'bah when praying.

The Masjid-ul-Aqsa is built on the site of the Jewish Temple. It is one of the holiest places in Islam.

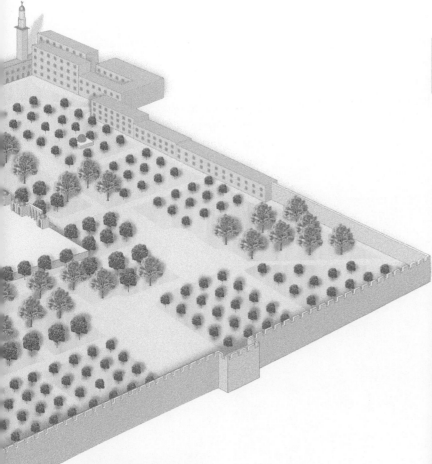

Ghawanima Minaret

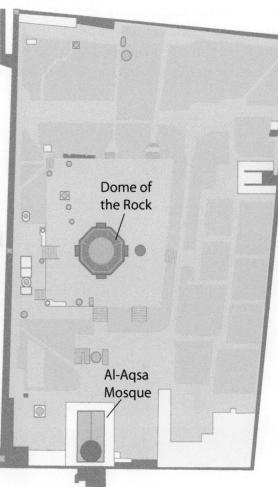

Dome of the Rock

Al-Aqsa Mosque

Activity A

Design and make a guidebook to the religious sites in Jerusalem. Include the Western Wall, the Church of the Holy Sepulchre and the Masjid-ul-Aqsa. You could research other holy sites in the city and add them to your booklet.

For each site, describe what there is to see, explain why it is there, and its importance for religious believers today. Try to include photographs and maps.

Activity B

The Masjid-ul-Aqsa is one of the holiest sites in Islam. Why is it so important for Muslims?

To answer this question, you will need to find out the details of the story of Muhammad's Night Journey and write an account of it. You will need to think about why the story is so important and how it is remembered today. You will also need to find out more about Mount Moriah, the hill on which the mosque is built.

Abrahamic faiths

Judaism, Christianity and Islam are together known as the Abrahamic faiths. All of them can trace their origins to one man: Ibrahim or Abraham (see page 6).

Ibrahim, and the prophets who came after him, have strong associations with Jerusalem, which is why Jerusalem is special to the three faiths. For Muslims, Ibrahim is known as the father of the prophets. He and his son, Isma'il, built the Ka'bah in Makkah.

The Ka'bah in Makkah is said to have been built by the first man, Adam, and rebuilt by Ibrahim and Isma'il.

Although Judaism, Christianity and Islam are distinctive religions, it is not surprising that they have much in common. They all teach:

- there is one God who created the universe and rules over it; who created human beings; who is omnipotent, omniscient, omnipresent and omnibenevolent
- God makes his will known to human beings through prophets
- God's will is contained in holy writings
- human beings have a duty to worship and obey God
- human beings should do good and avoid evil
- the world we know will end, and God will judge people according to their deeds and intentions.

Knowledge check

1 What is the Night Journey?

2 Why are Judaism, Christianity and Islam known as the Abrahamic faiths?

3 Which structure, sacred to Muslims, is said to have been built by Ibrahim and Isma'il?

4 Identify two teachings that are common to Judaism, Christianity and Islam.

Activity C

Produce a booklet or PowerPoint presentation on the central beliefs of the Abrahamic faiths. Make it in two sections: the first explaining the beliefs that are common to all three; the second outlining beliefs that are distinctive.

Activity D

Find out about what Judaism and Islam teach about Ibrahim (Abraham) preparing to sacrifice his son. Write accounts of the two stories, and then summarise the similarities and differences.

Why do you think the accounts are different?

2.4 Are all Muslims the same?

Learning objectives

You will ...
- find out why the Ummah divided
- learn about distinctive teachings and practices of the two groups
- evaluate different views about the two groups.

When Muhammad (pbuh) died in 632CE, there were about 100,000 Muslims. They now had to decide who was to be their leader.

Most of them said that the **Khalifah** (successor) of the Islamic nation should be the one who was best qualified to take on the role. The person they elected was Abu Bakr. Abu Bakr was a close friend of and adviser to the Prophet, and he was trusted by the people.

Sunnis

This group became known as Sunnis. The word Sunni means 'one who follows the **sunnah**' – the traditions of the Prophet. They claimed that, on his deathbed, Muhammad had asked Abu Bakr to lead the people in prayer. They took this to mean that Abu Bakr was to be the leader of all Muslims.

Shi'i

A minority of Muslims said that the Prophet had been appointed by God, so his successor should come from his family. They claimed that Muhammad's son-in-law and cousin, Ali, should be the Khalifah.

This group became known as Shi'i. The word Shi'ah means 'the party of supporters' (of Ali). They claimed that Muhammad had publicly appointed Ali to lead the Muslim nation.

Ali came to accept Abu Bakr's leadership, and, in time, he became Khalifah himself. After his death, the Shi'i continued to support leaders who were descendants of Muhammad, and did not accept the Sunni Khalifahs. Shi'ah leaders were known as imams, meaning guides.

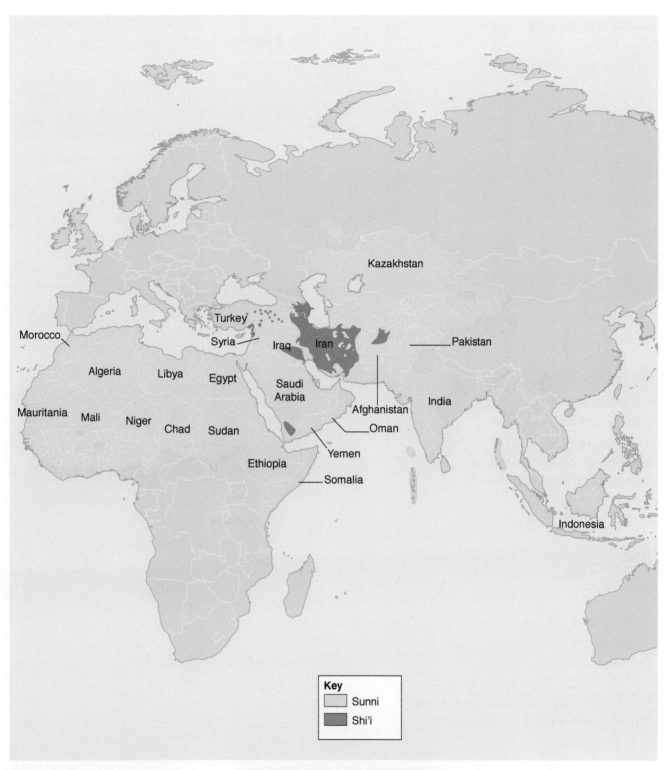

Key

Sunni
Shi'i

The map shows the distribution of Sunnis and Shi'i in parts of Europe, Africa and Asia. The division between Sunni and Shi'ah still exists today. About 85 per cent of the Muslim population is Sunni, and 15 per cent Shi'ah.

Knowledge check

1 What are the two groups of Muslims called?

2 Which group makes up most of the Muslim population?

3 Why did the Ummah split?

4 Who was the first Khalifah?

5 Who did the Shi'i think should be leader after Muhammad?

Sunnis and Shi'i share the same basic beliefs. However, disagreement about leadership of the Ummah has led to other differences.

THE MAHDI

There is a tradition in Islam that, before the Day of Judgement, the **Mahdi** will appear. He will be a descendant of Muhammad who will work with Isa (Jesus) to rid the world of evil. The idea of the Madhi is not a strong one among most Sunnis, but is very important to Shi'i. Some Shi'i believe that the twelfth Imam was hidden by Allah towards the end of the ninth century, and it will be he who returns at the end of time.

The Masjid Ali in Najaf, Iraq, is the resting place of Imam Ali, and is a place of pilgrimage for Shi'ah Muslims.

HADITH

The Hadith are the words and deeds of the Prophet as remembered by his friends and followers. Shi'i do not regard all of the Hadith as having the same authority. They give preference to those remembered by Muhammad's family and close associates, whereas Sunnis believe all the Hadith accounts are equally important.

THE IMAMS

Shi'ah Muslims believe that Ali and the eleven imams that followed him were not prophets (Muhammad was the last prophet), but were given the power to interpret the Qur'an and Hadith with Allah's authority. They are therefore regarded with great respect, and Shi'ah Muslims go on pilgrimages to their tombs.

SHAHADAH

The shi'ah Shahadah is different from the Sunni version. Shi'i add phrases to declare their beliefs about Ali: 'There is no god but Allah; Muhammad is the Messenger of Allah; Ali is the Friend of Allah, the Successor of the Messenger of Allah and his first Khalifah.'

SALAH

Some Shi'i combine the compulsory five prayers into three. Some place their forehead on a clay block (called mo'hr) rather than directly on the prayer mat.

Today, there is some tension between the Sunni and Shi'ah communities in Iraq, Pakistan and Afghanistan. Generally, however, the two communities do not allow their differences to split the Ummah, preferring to focus on their shared beliefs.

Activity A

Draw a chart to compare Sunni and Shi'ah teachings and practices. Your chart should show clearly the things that the two communities have in common, and those that are distinctive.

Activity B

1 Find out about the Shi'ah Remembrance of Muharram. Make a display to show what it commemorates, why it is important to Shi'ah, and the events that take place.

2 The end of the Remembrance of Muharram is marked by the Day of Ashura. Find out why this day is special for Sunni Muslims.

Activity C

The division between Sunni and Shi'ah Muslims came about because of a dispute about who should lead the Ummah. Sunnis said the leader should be elected; Shi'i said he should be a descendant of Prophet Muhammad.

What reasons would each group have for their point of view? Which do you most agree with?

Activity D

'The succession to Muhammad was a long time ago. Muslims should forget their differences and share the same beliefs, traditions and practices.'

1 Why might someone hold this point of view? Why might others disagree?

2 What is your view?

2.5 What do Muslims believe about death?

Learning objectives

You will ...
- find out about Muslim beliefs about death, judgement and the afterlife
- find out about what happens at Muslim funerals
- understand how Muslims prepare for death
- understand how Muslim funeral rituals are designed to help the dead.

Muslims believe that this life is a preparation for eternal life after death. Human beings choose what they say and do, and how they lead their lives. So, even though Allah knows what choices they will make, humans are responsible for their own actions. Their life beyond death depends on their actions in this life.

Islam teaches that, at the moment of death, angels will ask them if they believe in Allah and his Prophet. At that moment they know how their life will be judged.

Islam teaches that there will be a time when the sun and earth are destroyed, and the Day of Judgement arrives. The dead will rise to join the living, and God will present each person with their own book: a record of their good deeds and their bad deeds, which will be weighed.

> If the good outweighs the bad, even by one deed, the person goes to paradise: 'Whoever does good equal to the weight of an atom shall see it.'
>
> (Surah 99.7)

> A Muslim who has led a good life will be visited by beautiful angels who say: 'Fear not, nor grieve! But receive the good news of paradise which you have been promised!'
>
> (Surah 41.30)

> The wicked know that judgement will go against them: 'The record of everyone's deeds is set in place; and you will see the disbelieving criminals filled with fear because of what is in it, and they will say: "Alas, woe is ours! What is this record? It leaves out nothing, be it small or great, but everything is accounted."'
>
> (Surah 18.49)

> A wicked person will be visited by terrifying angels: 'If you could see when the angels take away the souls of those who disbelieve, they hit their faces and their backs, saying: "Taste the punishment of the blazing fire."'
>
> (Surah 8.50)

A Muslim funeral in India.

Islam teaches that the reward or punishment lasts for ever.

> *Those whose good deeds outweigh the bad will be led to paradise: 'You will be healthy and never fall sick, you will live and never die, you will be young and never age, you will be joyful and never feel miserable.'*
>
> (Hadith)

> *The wicked will be cast into hell: 'For those who disbelieve in their Lord is the punishment of hell. How evil a destination to arrive at! When they are cast into it, they will hear a rasping breath that sucks them in as it boils up.'*
>
> (Surah 67.6–7)

Knowledge check

1 According to Islam, what is the purpose of life?
2 What are people presented with on the Day of Judgement?

- When a Muslim is nearing the point of death, they will try to recite the Shahadah. They will also try to say, 'Allah, help me through the hardship and agony of death', as the Prophet is believed to have done.
- Relatives will recite passages from the Qur'an in the hope that Allah will be merciful. They will also say, 'There is no God but Allah', so that the dying person will not be confused about their faith.
- After death, the body is placed on a stretcher so that the head faces the Ka'bah in Makkah. Relatives of the same gender as the deceased wash the corpse three times using perfumed water.
- They then wrap it in a single piece of white cloth.

A Muslim funeral at a Muslim cemetery.

The funeral takes place the day after the death, if possible, and certainly within three days.

- The body is buried, never cremated, so it is ready for resurrection. It is placed so that the head faces the Ka'bah.
- At the graveside, mourners say funeral prayers – Salat-ul-Janaza (salah without rak'ahs) – to ask God to forgive the deceased, and they recite the first surah of the Qur'an.
- As the body is lowered into the ground, they say: *'We created you from earth, and we are returning you to it; and out of it, we will bring you forth a second time.'* (Surah 20.55)

Seven days after the funeral, relatives visit the grave as a mark of respect.

Knowledge check

1 What did Muhammad (pbuh) say before he died?
2 Why do relatives recite the Shahadah to a dying person?
3 Which way should a corpse's head face?
4 Why are Muslim corpses never cremated?

Activity A

Draw a flow chart to show Muslim beliefs and practices about death. Start your diagram with preparations for death, and end it with eternal reward or punishment.

Activity B

How do Muslim funeral rituals reflect beliefs about death and the afterlife?

Activity C

What can a Muslim do to be sure of earning a place in paradise?

Activity D

'There is no point to elaborate funeral arrangements. Once a person is dead, there is nothing the living can do to help them.'

1 How far do you agree with this statement?
2 Explain what a Muslim point of view might be.

The big assignment

Task

To create learning materials so that pupils in Years 4 and 5 can gain knowledge and understanding of Muslim beliefs and teachings.

Objectives

- To research Muslim teachings and beliefs.
- To use your knowledge, understanding and skills to pass on your learning to others.
- To devise appropriate learning activities for younger pupils.

Outcome

To produce a textbook with associated learning materials on Muslim beliefs.

You should include information about:

- Tawhid
- angels
- books
- messengers and prophets
- the Day of Judgement
- predestination
- life after death.

You should also give pupils opportunities to think about their own beliefs and things that are important to them.

Guidance

1. Work in groups of seven people. Each person should work on one belief.

2. Present information about the belief in ways that pupils in Years 4 and 5 (ages eight to ten) would understand.

3. Use colourful graphics and illustrations.

4. Create exercises and activities that will test pupils' knowledge and understanding, and allow them to practise skills.

5. Include opportunities for pupils to think about and express their own beliefs, views and opinions.

6. Children in Years 4 and 5 should be able to:
   - describe religious beliefs and see how they may affect someone's life
   - compare beliefs and practices between different groups
   - use religious words
   - give their own views on questions of life and death.

7. They should also be able to:
   - explain some religious words
   - make charts
   - do quizzes
   - pick out information.

8. Each member of the group should produce:
   - two pages of information and illustrations, and
   - associated activity and work sheets.

9. Pass completed work around the group so that it can be checked for accuracy, spelling, grammar and punctuation.

10. Add any new ideas.

11. You could present your work to teachers in a local primary school for them to assess and try out on their pupils.

Assessment

You will be assessed on:

✓ how well you use specialist vocabulary

✓ the accuracy of your accounts of Muslim teachings and beliefs

✓ your ability to show how beliefs affect the ways in which people live

✓ your ability to ask questions that trigger thoughts and ideas about the meaning of life.

3.1 What do Muslims believe about right and wrong?

Learning objectives

You will ...
- learn about Shari'ah
- study some examples of Shari'ah
- evaluate some examples of Shari'ah.

The way a Muslim lives is ruled by **Shari'ah**. Shari'ah means 'the Way', and refers to a way of life directed by the will of Allah.

'For each community we have set out a clear way of life and a complete system ... So compete with each other to do good works. You will all return to God, and he will then tell you what the differences are.'

(Surah 5.48)

So it is Shari'ah that tells Muslims what is right and wrong.

Shari'ah comes from two sources:
- the Qur'an and
- the Sunnah (the traditions that come from the Prophet).

Shi'i Muslims include the interpretations of the imams in the Sunnah.

Shari'ah guides every area of life. It can be divided into five branches. There are rules about:
- worship
- business
- manners and behaviour
- marriage and divorce
- crime and punishment.

marriage and divorce

manners and behaviour

crime and punishment

worship

business

Shar'iah

Shari'ah covers important aspects of human life.

Shari'ah does not just say what is right and what is wrong.
Human activities are put into five categories:

- compulsory
- recommended
- allowed
- discouraged
- forbidden.

- Some Muslim countries, like Saudi Arabia, have legal systems based on Shari'ah. Religious leaders interpret laws, not judges or politicians.

- Some Muslim countries, such as Pakistan, have legal systems that are influenced by Shari'ah. Politicians make laws and judges interpret them.

- Some Muslim countries, like Turkey, have legal systems that are not allowed to be influenced by religion. Shari'ah is limited to personal and family life.

Knowledge check

1 What does Shari'ah mean?
2 Where does Shari'ah come from?
3 Name one country that bases its laws on Shari'ah.
4 Name one Muslim country whose laws have nothing to do with Shari'ah.

Some countries have courts to settle disputes according to Shari'ah law. This one is in Pakistan.

Here are some examples from the Qur'an and Hadith about what is right and wrong.

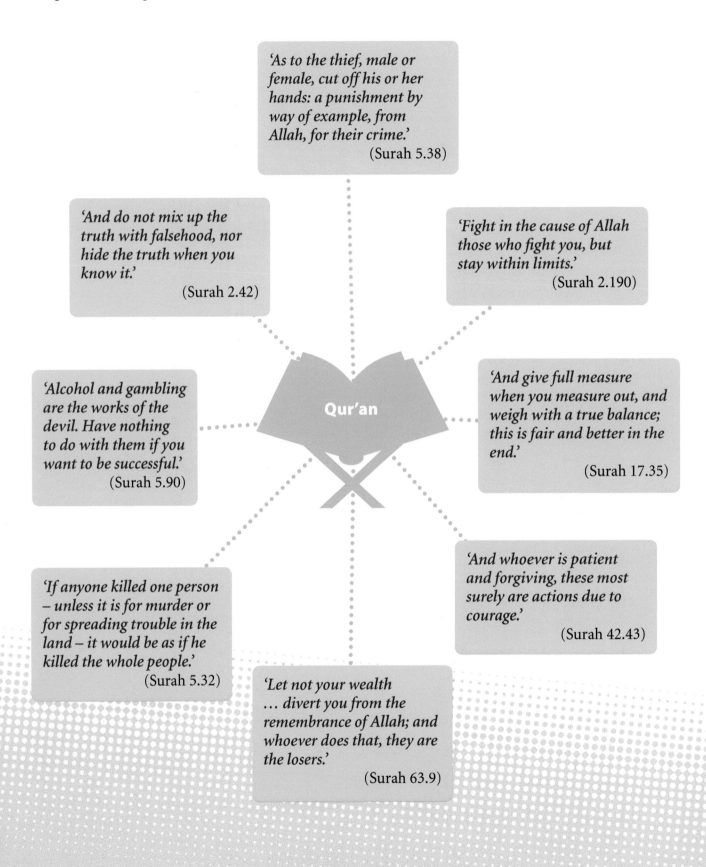

'As to the thief, male or female, cut off his or her hands: a punishment by way of example, from Allah, for their crime.'
(Surah 5.38)

'And do not mix up the truth with falsehood, nor hide the truth when you know it.'
(Surah 2.42)

'Fight in the cause of Allah those who fight you, but stay within limits.'
(Surah 2.190)

'Alcohol and gambling are the works of the devil. Have nothing to do with them if you want to be successful.'
(Surah 5.90)

Qur'an

'And give full measure when you measure out, and weigh with a true balance; this is fair and better in the end.'
(Surah 17.35)

'If anyone killed one person – unless it is for murder or for spreading trouble in the land – it would be as if he killed the whole people.'
(Surah 5.32)

'And whoever is patient and forgiving, these most surely are actions due to courage.'
(Surah 42.43)

'Let not your wealth … divert you from the remembrance of Allah; and whoever does that, they are the losers.'
(Surah 63.9)

No institution in Islam finds more favour with God than marriage.
(Hadith)

Let no man be in privacy with a woman who he is not married to, or Satan will be the third.
(Hadith)

Hadith

Cheerfulness and a good nature drive out hatred and bitterness.
(Hadith)

Do not hate one another and do not be jealous of one another, and be servants of Allah like brothers; and it is not lawful for a Muslim that he should break relations with his brother for more than three days.
(Hadith)

He is not of us who does not show kindness to our little ones and respect to our elders.
(Hadith)

Activity B

What does Shari'ah say about the following issues? Write one sentence on each.

- marriage
- theft
- war
- drinking alcohol
- hatred
- forgiving others
- lying
- the death penalty.

Activity A

Islam puts human behaviour into five categories: compulsory; recommended; allowed; discouraged; forbidden. Try to think of two sorts of behaviour that you would put in each category.

Activity D

'Laws that govern a nation should not be based on religion.'

1 What do you think? Back up your opinion with reasons.

2 What reasons would someone have for disagreeing with you?

Activity C

1 Read the quotations from the Qur'an and the Hadith carefully.

2 Choose three that you agree with and three that you disagree with. For each one, say why you agree or disagree, and give reasons and examples to back up your views.

3 Are there any teachings that are particularly difficult to follow in twenty-first-century Britain? Which ones? Why?

3.2 How do Muslims treat the world around them?

Learning objectives

You will ...
- learn Muslim teachings and beliefs about human responsibility for the environment
- understand the idea of stewardship
- understand why water is important in Islam
- learn how Muslims put their beliefs about the environment into practice
- interpret some quotations from the Qur'an.

Muslims believe that ...

God created everything that is on the earth.

God created the universe and the earth within it.

God is ruler of the earth, and has appointed human beings to be his deputy.

Human beings are responsible for everything that exists on planet Earth.

Human beings should not waste the earth's resources.

If human beings mistreat the earth, they will be questioned and punished in the next life.

The idea that God put human beings in charge of the earth with a responsibility to look after it is called **stewardship**. In Islam, human beings are called Khalifahs of the earth, because it is their job to manage and look after it.

What does the Qur'an teach about the environment?

'Corruption has flourished on land and sea as a result of people's actions and he will make them taste the consequences of some of their own actions so that they may turn back.'

(Surah 30.41)

'Do they not look at the earth – how many noble things of all kinds we have produced in it?'

(Surah 26.7)

'Lo! the squanderers were ever brothers of the devils, and the devil was ever ungrateful to his Lord.'

(Surah 17.27)

'Do you not see that God has made subject to you [humans] all that is on the earth?'

(Surah 22.65)

'He is the Originator of the heavens and the earth … He created all things.'

(Surah 6.101)

'Your Lord said to the angels: "Lo! I am about to place a viceroy on the earth."'

(Surah 2.30)

Water in Islam

Islam started in the desert regions of the Arabian Peninsula where water is a scarce commodity. For desert dwellers, it is the 'secret of life'. Islam discourages wasting anything, but wasting water is strictly forbidden. Water is seen as the most valuable commodity for all living things.

How do Muslims put their beliefs about the environment into practice?

In July 2009, 50 Muslim scholars met in Istanbul, Turkey, to approve a long-term plan for the Ummah to act on climate change. It is called the Muslim Seven-Year Action Plan on Climate Change 2010–17. This is their vision statement:
We envision a world that is environmentally safe for our children and the next generations; where all nations of all religions live in harmony with nature and enjoy justice and a fair share of God's bounties.

The Plan includes actions for:
- a Green Hajj, to make the Hajj a more environmentally friendly event by, for example, eliminating the use of plastic water bottles
- the construction of a Green Mosque, to showcase best practice in environmentally friendly heating, lighting and design, as a model for future mosque building
- publishing a Green Qur'an, using environmental principles and paper from sustainable sources.

Knowledge check

1 According to Islam, who is the ruler of the world?
2 What is the role of human beings?
3 What is stewardship?
4 Why is water so important to Muslims?

Activity A

1 Read the quotations from the Qur'an on page 55. Match them up with the sentences on page 54.
2 Now say which of the sentences and quotations you agree with, and which you disagree with.

Activity B

1 Water is essential for life; it can also kill. Write lists of all the ways in which water supports life, and ways that it can destroy it.
2 Put your ideas in the form of a poster. You could try to find some quotations from the Qur'an about water to include in your work.

Activity C

1 Read again Surah 30.41 on page 55. What do you think it means? Include examples of 'corruption … on land and sea as a result of people's actions' in your answer.
2 Explain how Muslims can 'turn back'.

Activity D

In Islam, human beings are said to be Khalifahs (stewards) of planet Earth. The word Khalifah is also used for the successors of Prophet Muhammad (pbuh), leaders of the Ummah (see Chapter 2.4).

What do the two roles have in common? To answer this question, you will need to conduct some research into the characteristics and functions of the leaders of the Ummah, and the qualities necessary to be a steward of God's creation.

3.3 What do Muslims believe about family life?

Learning objectives

You will ... • find out about some Islamic family values
• compare Islamic values with Western values
• consider some of the challenges some British teenage Muslims face in Britain.

RAJANI COMES TO ROXBURGH

Chapter 1:
The New Girl

Rajani sat down slowly. She was nervous to be in the company of the older girls on her first day at Roxburgh College. They seemed so different.

'Don't worry. We won't bite,' laughed one of them. She was called Kelly, and seemed to be the leader. Even though she was wearing school uniform, her skirt was very short and her shirt was very tight. 'My dad would kill me if I ever dressed like that,' thought Rajani.

'What are you staring at?' demanded Kelly.

'I'm sorry,' replied Rajani. 'I wasn't being rude. It's just that we don't wear clothes like that.'

'Who's "we"?' asked Becky, one of the other girls.

'I'm a Muslim,' said Rajani. 'My family originally came from Bangladesh, though I was born here, in England. In my religion, Islam, women wear loose-fitting clothes that don't show the shape of the body. So we wear trousers, like I am, or a long dress. And we usually cover our heads with a veil, like this one I'm wearing. It's called a **hijab**. Not all Muslim women wear them, but I do.'

'What on earth for?' asked Kelly.

'So as not to be seen as a sex-object. We want to be appreciated for who we are, not what we look like.'

'Please yourself!' laughed Kelly.

'So, what are you going to do when we have PE tomorrow?' This question came from Jess, who had not spoken up until now.

'I'll wear a tracksuit. Strictly speaking, Muslims do not agree with schools where boys and girls are taught together, but there's not much you can do about that in England. In any case, we don't do PE with the boys in this school, do we?'

'No,' said Jess. 'But we do all our other lessons with them. What are you going to do about Sex and Relationships Ed?'

'I don't think my parents will approve of it. They will probably withdraw me from it. We think that sex and relationships should be taught about in the family. And we don't approve of sex before marriage. In fact, Muslims don't really approve of having boyfriends or girlfriends.'

'What?' Becky spluttered incredulously. 'Who do you hang around with in the evenings, then?'

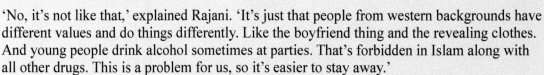

'I tend to stay at home with my family. When I say my family, I don't mean just my mum and dad and brothers and sister. My dad's parents live with us, as well. And his brother lives in our road with his wife and children, so there are always plenty of people around. But my parents wouldn't like me to go to a party, say, with non-Muslims.'

'Isn't that a bit racist?' said Jess.

'No, it's not like that,' explained Rajani. 'It's just that people from western backgrounds have different values and do things differently. Like the boyfriend thing and the revealing clothes. And young people drink alcohol sometimes at parties. That's forbidden in Islam along with all other drugs. This is a problem for us, so it's easier to stay away.'

'So you just do what your parents tell you? Doesn't it get boring?' enquired Kelly.

'Not at all. We have lots of parties, particularly when other family members come to stay, with lots of good food.'

'What sort of food? Curries and that?' asked Becky.

'That sort of thing, yes,' said Rajani. 'That's how my mum was taught to cook when she was a girl in Bangladesh.'

'What's wrong with good old eggs and bacon?' teased Becky.

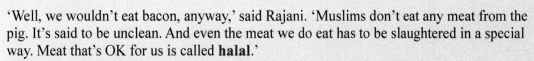

'Well, we wouldn't eat bacon, anyway,' said Rajani. 'Muslims don't eat any meat from the pig. It's said to be unclean. And even the meat we do eat has to be slaughtered in a special way. Meat that's OK for us is called **halal**.'

'Blimey!' exclaimed Jess. 'How do you manage at lunchtime in school?'

'I bring a packed lunch. You see, it's not just meat from the pig. A lot of food like crisps, biscuits, chocolate and ice-cream might have pork fat in it. You have to be very careful!'

'Pig fat in chocolate? That's gross!' Jess gasped. 'I'm not touching that again!'

Rajani looked at her watch. 'Hey, look at the time. I'm sorry, girls – the bell will be going in ten minutes, and I've got to say my prayers.'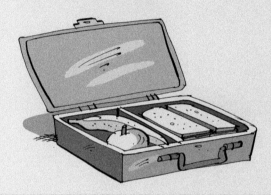

'You've got to what?' asked Kelly. But Rajani was rushing away.

'See you later,' she called over her shoulder.

'Yeah. See you later,' said the others.

Knowledge check

1 What is a hijab?

2 Why do Muslim women wear loose-fitting clothes?

3 Why are Rajani's parents likely to withdraw her from the school's Sex and Relationships Education programme?

4 What is halal meat?

Activity A

1 Imagine you are a Muslim child attending a school in the UK where nearly all of the pupils are white British. What sorts of problems might this present for you?

2 Write a problem page for a Muslim teenagers' magazine. Write two or three letters from young Muslims outlining their difficulties, and answer them by giving advice.

Activity B

Write Chapter 2 of *Rajani Comes to Roxburgh*. In this chapter, Rajani comes home after school and tells her parents and grandparents about her day.

Make sure you include the reactions of the older generations to what Rajani has to say about her new friends and their lifestyle.

Activity C

Many Muslim parents arrange marriage partners for their children. Find out more about the different ways this may be done.

Are arranged marriages a good idea? Present arguments for and against, giving reasons. What is your opinion?

Activity D

Think about how life may be different for a teenage Muslim living in Britain compared with one from a Muslim country. Write two portraits: one of a British Muslim and the other of a Muslim in an Islamic country.

3.4 What do Muslims believe about money?

Learning objectives

You will ...
- find out what Islam teaches about money
- understand how Muslims use money
- apply Muslim teachings about money to authentic situations.

The strange thing about money is that we value it because of what it is worth to us. But actually, money is worth nothing in itself. It only has worth if you can buy something with it. A ten-pound note is only a small piece of paper. If you were stranded on a desert island, its only use would be to help you light a fire. Money is a means of exchange, a way of comparing the value of different things.

Muslim teachings about money are all based on the idea that money has no value in itself. What is important is what you do with it.

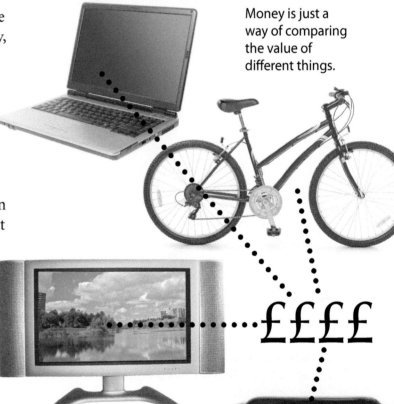

Money is just a way of comparing the value of different things.

Interest

'Allah will deprive usury (charging interest) of all blessing, but will give increase for deeds of charity.'

(Surah 2. 276)

Islam teaches that, because money is worth nothing in itself, you cannot make money out of it. You can only make money out of trading. So Muslims do not charge interest when they lend money. Shari'ah forbids it.

Normally, if you want to buy a house or a car, you borrow the money from a bank. You pay the bank back the money you have borrowed over a period of time, and the bank charges interest on the loan. So you may end up paying back twice what you borrowed.

If you go to an Islamic bank wanting to buy a house or a car, the bank will buy it for you, then sell it to you for more than they paid for it. They will then lend you the money, interest-free, to pay them for it. In this way, the bank makes money out of the property, not out of the loan.

Zakah

'You shall give to relatives, the poor, the needy, and to travellers.'

(Surah 17.26)

Zakah is the third of the Five Pillars of Islam. It is the practice of giving money to charity. The sum a person gives amounts to 2.5 per cent of their surplus wealth, that is whatever they have left over after essential expenditure. It is paid once a year (often people like to pay during the month of Ramadan), and distributed among the poor and needy. Because it is one of the Pillars, zakah is a compulsory payment. Muslims see it as a way of ridding themselves of greed and selfishness.

Earning money

The flesh and body that is raised on unlawful sustenance shall not enter Paradise.

(Hadith)

Muslims will try to earn a living in a way that fits in with Islamic principles. They should not work as money lenders, for example, or manufacture alcoholic drinks. Muslims will try to work to benefit others and not cause harm. So teaching, nursing or the law are professions that they may wish to work in.

Knowledge check

1 What does Islam teach about lending money?

2 What is zakah?

3 How much is zakah?

4 Suggest a job that would be good for a Muslim to have.

5 Suggest a job that a Muslim should not have.

Activity A

Think of two or three jobs that would be good for a Muslim to have. Create a newspaper page with recruitment advertisements for these jobs. Write the advertisements in such a way that they would appeal to Muslims.

Activity B

Design a home page for an Islamic charity's website to encourage Muslims to give their zakah to it. You should include an explanation of why zakah is paid, and information about the kind of work your organisation does and why it does it.

Activity C

'Zakah should only go towards helping Muslims.'

1 Do you agree with this statement? What reasons would you give for your opinion?

2 Why might someone disagree with you?

Activity D

Shi'ah Muslims have a different way of applying zakah from Sunnis, and make a further payment called khums. In addition, all Muslims try to pay sadaqah, which is voluntary charity.

1 Find out more about different interpretations of zakah, khums and sadaqah, and make a fact file on charity and Islam.

2 Do you agree that all religious people should be required to give to charity?

3.5 What do Muslims believe about war and peace?

Learning objectives

You will ...
- learn about jihad
- understand how Muslims practise the Greater Jihad
- understand the conditions for fighting a jihad
- evaluate jihad.

Jihad

Jihad is an Arabic word that means 'striving' or 'struggle'. Muslims use it to apply to any activity a person does because of the love of Allah. Jihad involves challenging yourself, making an effort and stretching your capabilities to achieve something great. This sort of jihad is often called the Greater Jihad or Inner Jihad.

So jihad means sometimes going against the easy option and doing what is difficult. Muhammad (pbuh) said that the Greater Jihad is:
- making an extra effort; for example, learning the Qur'an to become a hafiz
- forgiving someone when they have done you a terrible wrong
- sacrificing what is valuable to you to help someone else.

Military Jihad

The word jihad is sometimes used when Muslims go to war, especially if it is for the honour of Islam. Some Muslims call this the Lesser Jihad. The British press tends to use the word only when a Muslim country goes to war. But the Prophet Muhammad said, 'The person who struggles (*jihad*) so that Allah's word is supreme is the one serving Allah's cause.' (Hadith)

So if Muslims fight against forces that go against Islam, they may call it a jihad. A Muslim who struggles in such a way is called a **mujahid** (plural: mujahidin).

The purpose of military jihad is to bring peace, but it can only be fought in certain circumstances:
- in self-defence
- in defence of a country
- to fight against a cruel government
- to fight against injustice.

There are strict rules for fighting a jihad:
- It must have the authority of a religious leader.
- It must be fought for the cause of Allah.
- It must bring about good.
- It must be the last resort.
- It should never be fought to gain land.
- Killing must be targeted against enemy forces.
- Innocent people should not suffer.
- The natural environment should be protected.

Knowledge check

1 What does jihad mean?

2 What is the Greater Jihad?

3 What is the Lesser Jihad?

4 Why might Muslims go to war?

5 What is a Muslim who fights in a jihad called?

Members of the Jamiat-e Islami, mujahidin who fought against Soviet Russian invaders of Afghanistan in the 1970s, and more recently against the Taliban.

Activity A

1 Look through this book to find examples of practising the Greater Jihad. You could present your findings in a PowerPoint presentation or a booklet. Remember to explain why each example involved struggle and striving.

2 Think of times when you have challenged yourself or 'gone the extra mile' to achieve something great. Include these in your presentation.

Activity B

Imagine you are a television reporter interviewing a mujahid who is fighting against a foreign invader. Write up the interview, in which you try to find out how he can justify fighting and killing.

Activity C

'You cannot be religious and go to war.'

Draw a mind map to show your thoughts about this statement. You should include reasons why some people would agree with it, and reasons why some would disagree. You should also present information on Muslim teachings about jihad, and your own point of view.

Activity D

Some Muslims are pacifists: this means they believe that war and violence are never right. Khan Abdul Ghaffar Khan was a Muslim pacifist.

1 Find out about his life, his beliefs about non-violence, and how he put his beliefs into practice.

2 Write a report called 'How Khan Abdul Ghaffar Khan fought the Greater Jihad'.

Some people make generalisations about Muslims like these:

> Muslim parents force their children into marriages.

> All Muslims support terrorism.

> Muslims treat women like second-class citizens.

> British Muslims feel no loyalty to Britain.

> All terrorists are Muslims.

> Muslims hate non-Muslims.

The word '**Islamophobia**' has been around for over twenty years, but its use has become more common since the acts of terrorism that happened on 11 September 2001 (9/11).

On that day, nineteen men hijacked four passenger aircraft in America. They deliberately crashed the planes, killing themselves and almost 3000 victims. The hijackers were all Muslims.

On 7 July 2005, four men detonated bombs on public transport in London, killing themselves and 52 others, and injuring about 700. The suicide bombers were Muslims.

These and other similar attacks have led some people to believe that all Muslims approve of acts of terrorism against non-Muslims. Some go further, and imagine that Muslims have no values in common with other cultures, and that British Muslims have no wish to be a part of British society. As a result, Muslims and their property have been attacked.

A popular British daily newspaper claimed that two British banks had removed piggy banks from their promotional material to avoid offending Muslim customers. (Remember, pork is forbidden in Islam.) The story was completely untrue.

This book is about the beliefs, values and actions of moderate Islam, practised by the vast majority of Muslims. Extremists include a small minority who support terrorism. Some moderates would say that extremists have misunderstood Islam.

In an analysis of 974 newspaper stories about Muslims, a survey which was taken on 7 July 2008 found that:
- 36 per cent were about terrorism
- 22 per cent highlighted differences between Islamic and British cultures
- references to extremists outnumbered references to moderates by 17 to 1.

Only 5 per cent of the stories were about problems facing British Muslims.

The Muslim Council of Britain represents over 500 Muslim groups and is the largest Muslim representative organisation in the UK. In 2007 it stated: 'Those who seek to deliberately kill or maim innocent people are the enemies of all of us. There is no cause whatsoever that could possibly justify such barbarity. Those who engage in such murderous actions and those that provide support for them are the enemies of all, Muslims and non-Muslims, and they stand against our shared values in the UK.'

Islamophobia A fear or hatred of Islam and Muslims.
Extremism A tendency to have beliefs or opinions that are considered to be extremely unreasonable by most people.
Moderate Holding beliefs and values that are accepted as reasonable by most people.

Knowledge check

1 What is Islamophobia?
2 What does moderate mean when referring to religion?
3 Why do some people have a fear of Islam?
4 Give two examples of Islamophobic acts.

Activity A

Historically, Muslims have contributed greatly to human knowledge, and our lives are still influenced by Islamic innovations today. Muslims have given us words, invented products, made discoveries in science and mathematics, and introduced engineering techniques.

Find out about ways in which Muslims have advanced human civilisation. Present your findings to the rest of the class.

Activity B

Make a display for a multi-use space in your school, for example the Learning Resources Centre, if you have one. Your display should raise awareness of Islamophobia, and contain photographs, headlines and articles from newspapers, magazines and websites that show Islam and Muslims in a positive light.

Activity C

What can schools do to reduce Islamophobia? Think about what could be done both in and out of lessons. Write a report on your ideas.

Activity D

Muslims began to settle in the United Kingdom in the nineteenth century, and the first British mosque was established in Cardiff in 1860. Find out about the history of Muslims in Britain till the present day. How far are Muslims part of British culture and society? Give examples to illustrate your answer.

The big assignment

Task

To produce a magazine for teenage Muslims that will teach them about Islamic views on right and wrong in the modern world.

Objectives

- To research Muslim teachings on moral issues.
- To find examples of moral issues in the media.
- To link media articles with Muslim teachings.
- To present your views on the issues.

Outcome

To produce a magazine that could guide Muslim teenagers in Islamic teachings about a range of moral issues by using examples from contemporary media.

You should include information about:

- family life
- money and celebrity
- the environment
- war
- terrorism
- prejudice.

You should include stories and articles from newspapers, magazines and television channels about these issues, and explain what Islam teaches about them.

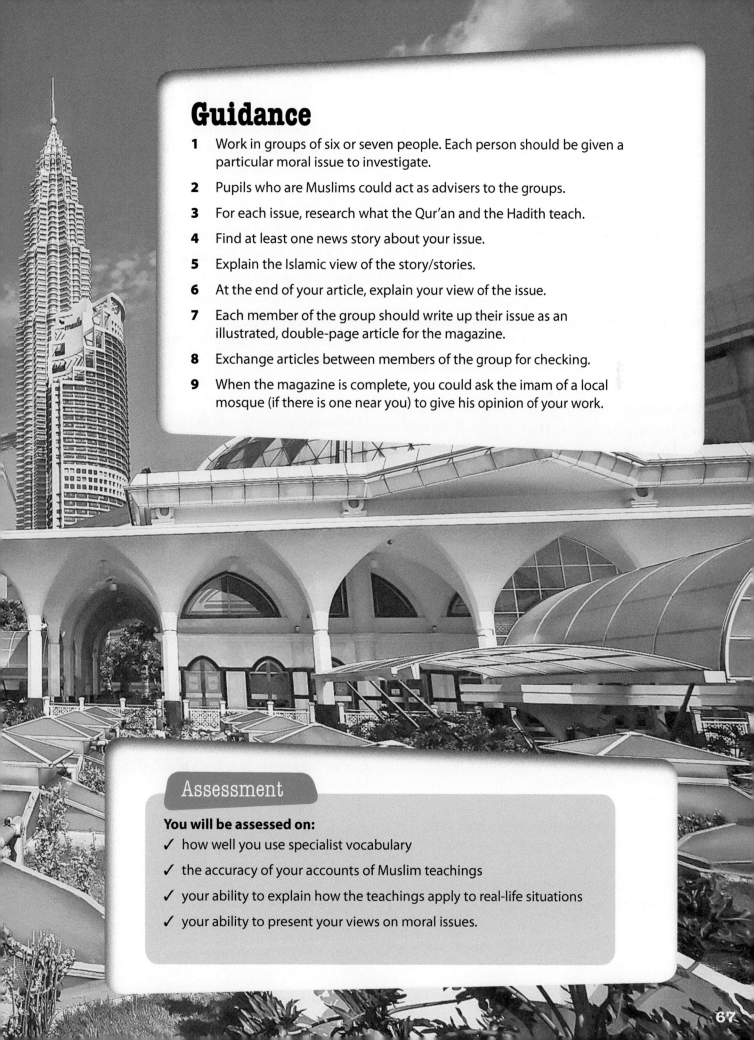

Guidance

1 Work in groups of six or seven people. Each person should be given a particular moral issue to investigate.

2 Pupils who are Muslims could act as advisers to the groups.

3 For each issue, research what the Qur'an and the Hadith teach.

4 Find at least one news story about your issue.

5 Explain the Islamic view of the story/stories.

6 At the end of your article, explain your view of the issue.

7 Each member of the group should write up their issue as an illustrated, double-page article for the magazine.

8 Exchange articles between members of the group for checking.

9 When the magazine is complete, you could ask the imam of a local mosque (if there is one near you) to give his opinion of your work.

Assessment

You will be assessed on:

✓ how well you use specialist vocabulary

✓ the accuracy of your accounts of Muslim teachings

✓ your ability to explain how the teachings apply to real-life situations

✓ your ability to present your views on moral issues.

Glossary

Adhan Call to prayer.

Allah Arabic word used by Muslims to refer to God. It means The God.

Extremism A tendency to have beliefs or opinions that are considered to be extremely unreasonable by most people.

Fard Compulsory duty.

Five Pillars of Islam Compulsory acts of worship.

Hadith Sayings and actions of Prophet Muhammad (pbuh).

Hafiz A person who has learnt the Qur'an by heart.

Hajj Annual pilgrimage to Makkah. (One of the Five Pillars of Islam.)

Hijab Veil or headscarf worn by many Muslim women.

Hijrah Departure from Makkah to Madinah by Prophet Muhammad in 622CE.

Id-ul-Adha Celebration of the sacrifice.

Id-ul-Fitr (pronounced *Eed*) Celebration of finishing the fast at the end of Ramadan.

Iftar The evening meal when Muslims break their fast during Ramadan.

Ihram The conditions of performing Hajj; particularly two pieces of white cloth worn by men.

Imam Leader of prayers. In Shi'ah Islam, Ali and his successors.

Islamophobia A fear or hatred of Islam and Muslims.

Jihad Individual spiritual effort or struggle. Also, often used to refer to military defence of the Ummah.

Jumu'ah prayers Weekly communal salah, performed after midday on Fridays.

Ka'bah Cube-shaped building in the Haram Mosque in Makkah, believed to be the House of God.

Khalifah Successor, steward, vice-regent.

Mahdi One who will appear at the end of time to lead the Ummah and restore justice.

Masjid Arabic word for mosque.

Mihrab Alcove in the wall of a mosque indicating the Qiblah and the place where the imam stands to pray.

Minaret Tower attached to a mosque, from the top of which the adhan is called.

Minbar A small staircase in a mosque, a pulpit from which the imam delivers his sermon or speech.

Moderate Holding beliefs and values that are accepted as reasonable by most people.

Mosque Islamic place of worship.

Omnibenevolent Perfectly good.

Omnipotent All powerful.

Omnipresent Always present.

Omniscient All knowing.

Predestined Prearranged, decided in advance.

Prophet Those chosen by God to teach his message to human beings.

Qiblah The direction Muslims face when praying, indicated by the Mihrab in the qiblah wall of a mosque.

Qur'an The Muslim holy book revealed to Muhammad.

Rak'ah A unit of prayer.

Ramadan Ninth month of the Islamic calendar, during which Muslims fast during daylight hours.

Salah Compulsory prayer (the second of the Five Pillars of Islam).

Sawm Fasting during daylight hours.

Sa'y Running between two hills (one of the rituals of the Hajj).

Shahadah Islamic statement of faith.

Shari'ah Islamic law, based on the Qur'an and Sunnah.

Shi'ah The group of followers of Ali (the fourth Sunni Khalifah) and the eleven imams as successors to Prophet Muhammad (pbuh).

Stewardship Responsibility for looking after the things God has created.

Sunnah Customs and traditions of Prophet Muhammad, taken from the Hadith.

Sunni Muslims who recognise the first four Khalifah as successors to Prophet Muhammad.

Surah Arabic name for a chapter of the Qur'an.

Tawaf Walking round the Kab'ah (one of the rituals of the Hajj).

Tawhid The oneness of Allah.

Ummah The community of Muslims throughout the world.

Washing area Part of a mosque used for wudu.

Wudu Ritual washing before salah.

Zakah Payment made annually under Islamic law (one of the Five Pillars of Islam).

Index

Acknowledgements

The Author and Publishers would like to thank the Chair of the Education Committee of the Muslim Council of Britain, Sheikh Dr Hojjat Ramzy for advising them on the content of this book.

The Publishers would like to thank the following for permission to reproduce copyright material:

Photo credits
p.4 *t* © Tjui Tjioe – Fotolia, *c* © Gideon Mendel/Corbis, *b* © Tjui Tjioe – Fotolia; **p.8** © Stock Master – Fotolia; **p.11** © Paul Wooton Associates; **p.13** © Peter Macdiarmid/Getty Images; **p.17** © Kazuyoshi Nomachi/Corbis; **p.19** © Al-Hidaayah Travel Ltd. Reproduced with permission; **p.21** © Kazuyoshi Nomachi/Corbis; **pp.24–25** © Andrew Fox/Corbis; **p.27** © Pattarasiri Virayasiri – Fotolia; **pp.28–29** © Mustafa Ozer/AFP/Getty Images; **p.31** © Photononstop/SuperStock; **p.32** © Art Directors & TRIP/Alamy; **pp.34–35** © A. Hyman Photography/Getty Images; **pp.38–39** © ayazad – Fotolia; **pp.42–43** © Caroline Penn/Corbis; **p.45** © 2011 epa/photolibrary.com; **p.46** © 2011 Don Arnold/Getty Images; **pp.48–49** © Konstantin Kalishko – Fotolia; **p.51** © Rashid Iqbal/epa/Corbis; **p.54** © NASA Goddard Space Flight Center (NASA-GSFC); **p.60** *t* © Fatman73 – Fotolia, *ct* © Julián Rovagnati – Fotolia, *cb* © Nguyen Thai – Fotolia, *b* © AP/Press Association Images; **p.63** © Julien Chatelin/Rex Features; **p.64** © overthehill – Fotolia; **pp.66–67** © Shirley – Fotolia.

Acknowledgements
p.20 Adam Yosef and BBC Birmingham for the quote from the BBC website.

Every effort has been made to trace all copyright holders, but if any have been inadvertently overlooked the Publishers will be pleased to make the necessary arrangements at the first opportunity.